KEEP CHASING

CW00434994

THIRD TIME TRULY

LOVING UNCONDITIONALLY

Jason thomson

To ANNA
FOR ALL THE WORDS
WE HAVE TO SAY, WHAT
WE WRITE DOWN WON'T
GO AWAY   Love Jason x

Third Time Truly Loving Unconditionally

Authors Notes

This book is entirely fictional, apart from the facts, in addition with what is heartfelt. Superstition was left behind in order for superstition to play its part. No part of this publication may be copied without the authors permission.

Third Time Truly Loving Unconditionally

Dedication

*This is my third book of lingering poems,
capturing in words each expression of experience,
the joy and anguish of emotions that lingered on,
until they found their rightful resting place,
inside these pages.*

*Hope they help to console and heal, with their authenticity and love. May their message spread like
wild flowers, across the pastures, of one's heart,
and bring back memories of a higher love,
Our love for one another. Our soul family.*

*I would like to dedicate this book to my brothers,
my family my wonderful friends who inspired me
along my journey. To everyone who reads this
book and those who don't, I hope your days are
filled with love.*

BAT (Book One)

ELEPHANT (Book Two)

LION (Book Three)

B.E.L

When a bell rings,
An angel grows wings.

Table of Contents

Authenticity

With a spark of inspiration,
We begin each creation,
In our world of interpretation,
We fit in,
To begin where we begin.

Within this age,
Of black mirror deception,
Of unmerciful mechanical production,
Authenticity hardly gets a whiff,
Of uniqueness,
Of original thought,
It's as if,
What's sought after is rarely taught.

There's a build up,
Of obligations,
Of expectations,
Of bewilderment and regrets,
Like we're constructing Ikea cabinets,
While waiting for the instructions.

How can we do this,
Come on,
There's no real acquirable,
Short cuts,
No real plausible,
Ifs or buts,
If we only did this,
Or we only did that,
Throw away words,
Within our throw away chat.

So many irresponsible,
Agreeable answers,
To whatever somebody asks,
Avoiding acquiring new skills,
For any feasible task.

What's the use,
Of us frantically finding,
Every feeble excuse,
What's written inside this book,
Is not written to conduce,
By tying a noose,
Around our ambiguous ambitions,
Before we begin to even take a look.

Can we start pulling back the curtains,
To eventually reveal,
Who's running this symbolic show,
Can we depart and go,
Running up a workaholic hill,
To reveal,
There's no goodwill,
From what's going on,
Down below.

This dark plague of corruption,
Without the slightest interruption,
The band of the suppressed,
Keeps playing on,
Like everyone is unremitting,
Without admitting,
They were in the wrong.

No one takes responsibility,
After years of hard hostility,
Scarred by so much fear,
It's been going on too long,
Without integrity.

The virtuous vultures,
Of the fakes' cancel culture,
Are dropping hard like frozen flakes,
How can we learn,
Without concern,
From our plethora of mistakes?

Still we make excuses,
It's hard enough,
To know what's real,
But we know too well,
That we're no one's personnel.

We should've finished,
The books we started,
We should've hugged,
Before we parted.

Authenticity without history,
Playing out with synchronicity,
Chapter and verse,
It couldn't get any worse.

Third time lucky,
Loving unconditionally,
Questioning authority,
With our own kind,
Of authenticity.

When You Know, You Know

Breaking free from our routines,
From where we've been,
Those distant days,
Life's colossal circus of distractions,
Away from what we know,
While holding onto every memory,
In the confection jar of one's mind,
Laying tasteless,
In its frenzy.

We're like some old depleting battery,
Powering the old machine,
The old decrees,
There's just no natural nationality,
Powers and principalities,
There's no loyalty in royalty.

What difference does it make,
What's happening now,
Didn't happen before,
After all the wisdom has been said,
Does it remove the suffering in one's head?

Trying to wipe the slate clean,
Brain cells dying,
Knowing nothing,
Slaves to the silver screen,
A world inside another world.

Infant to the ancient,
Have the ability to take it in their stride,
But are we tired of being patient,
After all the tears we've cried,
It takes centuries,
For a river to find its bed,
It takes the longest time,
For sad memories to leave our head.

Resilient in our ability,
To handle uncomfortability,
We have to keep on going,
Past the premise of suppose,
Motion keeps on forever flowing,
Searching for life everywhere it goes,
Sooner or later,
It's either now or never,
Whether or not,
It's written down in poetry or prose.

Just when we think we know,
We never really know the absolute,
Moving forward without reversibility,
Forward with responsibility,
With the sweetest dilemmas,
Wearing God's armour,
The armour of compatibility,
Love is in need of love,
In all its availability.

Love's tolerance,
Is so complete,
Packed full with feelings,
Igniting our greatest sense of being,
Beg a moment,
Steal a moment,
Borrow what you need to borrow,
Till that day of reuniting,
In our forever tomorrow,
Till that day when you know,
You know.

Why?

Why don't we think why,
Think to ask why,
To search for a broader picture,
When clarities are not clear,
Weird gets itself wired to weird,
When the truth is censored.

What's left out there,
To be feared,
Why are we really here,
If we lay down and die,
Every day ends in ay,
For us to finally question why,
Caught between what's frightening,
And what we're fighting,
Every musketeer,
To every puppeteer.

Why do we make try,
After try,
Rewriting what is meant for us,
Won't make it pass us by,
Why are some deemed rich,
While others are deemed poor,
What is it that we are waiting for,
Another dystopian switch,
For us to applaud,
As it switches on their continuing fraud?

Why are we being ruled, robbed and caged,
What's really happening,
Behind events that are staged,
Like climate change and global warming,
Why isn't it dawning,
That we're becoming colder,
As division after division,
Keeps on spalling,
Now there's a calling,
For us to stand together,
Shoulder to shoulder.

We've had so much confusion,
So much coercion,
It's the same old story,
When the wools pulled over our eyes,
Surprise after surprise,
That we've been too blind to see,
Builds up to the very next catastrophe.

Why do we practice avoidance,
Until we lose touch,
Why do we think ourselves important,
But dislike ourselves so much?

Why do we always say always,
When always makes promises,
It never keeps,
Why do we jump to conclusions,
Before our own hearts leap?

What is war really for,
Why would any sane body,
Consider more,
Why don't we flee,
From the first signs of fate,
Why would we take the knee,
To a totalitarian state,
Why don't we the people come together,
In our solidarity instead of hate?

Why don't we give ourselves time to think,
Before we consent,
Why do our egos,
Dive us down into the depths,
Of blasphemy,
Why do we live with so much anxiety?

Why don't we change,
Our behaviour,
Our ways of behaving,
Why don't we question,
The reasons we're ageing,
The very next bandwagon,
The one we all jump on,
Why don't we question,
The lie behind contagion?

Why do we go out on a wing and a prayer,
Before every ordeal,
Why don't we prepare,
Why do we trust,
Those who we believe we know,
But we will never meet,
Why do we live in a world,
That is full of deceit?

Why do we justify,
Without questioning why,
Why is there a good,
In our goodbye,
Without any reply?

Turning Our Hearts Around

Engulfed in love's lave,
Wave after wave,
Of romantic obsession,
A promise's worth,
Is rarely spoken.

Our words,
Are our deeds,
Who in their life needs,
False hope,
It's easy to cope,
In a place where the truth never lies,
Scary people do scary things,
Without any compromise.

There's so much more to love,
Than rings,
On fingers,
There's so much more to love,
Than poems,
That linger.

It's hard to convince anyone,
That love has arrived,
If they're waiting for love,
To be identified.

Without any reprieve,
Love doesn't just set up,
And then leave,
Demanding the price of a promise's worth,
Moving Heaven and Earth.

Bare foot on the ground,
Putting everything out there,
Arms spreading wider,
Than they've been apart,
Trying to turn,
Around your heart.

We've got to be,
Creating something,
It's not like we're still standing,
Where we once stood,
We've got to be moving on,
We will never know what's really lost,
Until it's been found immured in a memory,
That's misunderstood.

There's not one face in a crowd,
That's never seen tears,
That doesn't know what it is to love and go without,
Throughout the years.

There's sunshine behind every cloud,
We'll miss that perfect smile,
If we keep looking for plaque,
We'll never hit a home run,
Without a big whack,
Then it hits us right between the eyes,
We're stronger,
Than we believe we are,
There's love in your eyes,
That's growing greater.

Throughout each century,
No one goes unloved,
In each heart there is plenty,
What is the likelihood,
That love's always found,
Without any spin,
We must never give in,
We've come so far,
Good will in turn,
Do good,
Turning our hearts around.

Victim Mode

It's all about choices,
Which choices we make,
Which path we take.

Freely writing is the pen,
Released from its penitentiary,
Something's bound to explode,
After being bound so tightly.

Episode after episode,
The psychological,
Affects what's biological,
If we keep on relaying our woes,
In victim mode.

Slaves to the system,
Set in their programs,
And conditions,
The man made materialistic world,
Materialises through trickery and illusions.

When will we realise,
One day it's going to hit us,
Like a transparent,
Double decker bus,
It will become apparent,
That no one knows you,
Better than you.

When will we recognise,
The pain and suffering,
Our World's been in,
Can we take,
The empath's road of compromise,
To find a good place to be,
Be our own beneficiary,
Physically and mentally,
We are our own trustees.

The only one,
That is going to save you,
Is you,
To off load some mental load,
Don't let yourself forever ferment,
In victim mode.

As we keep moving on,
What conscious steps are we taking,
We can't just download,
Another app for apprehension.

We can't go on losing,
All our change,
Before it's spent,
What extent,
Will we go to,
Can we change our own intent,
From victim mode?

Daily we're provided,
With another program,
To control our environment,
Within our daily association,
With interaction.

Something's bound to snap,
With so much high tension,
But everything's alright,
In spite of those things,
We're too scared to mention.

This material world we live in,
Gets under the skin,
Toxin after toxin,
Until we're boxed in,
With ignorance and self-hate,
This false ego has taken years,
Reaching out it's hands of fate,
Reaching this state,
But it's never too late.

You're not that dumb,
You're saviours come,
To rip off the gauze,
From the root cause,
Freeing ourselves,
From the humongous jaws,
Of victim mode.

One Plus Two

The whole time,
Time's been an illusion,
An artificial affliction,
Of the third dimension.

It's just a superficial construct,
Make of it whatever you will,
From the connoisseurs,
To the amateurs,
Time still stands still,
Without the numbers,
Times not even real.

Mathematics is odd,
In its conspiracy circus,
Used to obtain,
Or achieve,
Patterns emerge to sustain,
Or deceive.

What are we to anyone,
What are they to us,
What do we believe,
Every one completes everyone,
Before everyone leaves?

Let's do the maths,
Two's company,
But three's a crowd,
What sums up a community,
For crying out loud?

We're battling with trust and mistrust
The World's in distress,
Who are we trying to impress,
Monogamy to bigamy,
To none the less.

Everyone's a comparison,
Not to be outdone,
The proof is in prosperity's pudding,
Nobody's won,
While drowning in booze,
Where is the love,
Let love be your muse.

In the crystal ball of destiny,
We choose what's left of eternity,
What's concealed is opened,
When the sums just don't add up,
We keep regurgitating,
What we are digesting,
If we keep on drinking,
From the Devil's cup.

We're trying to make something work,
That we don't comprehend,
Trust is such a big word,
Followed by honesty,
Can we really trust those,
Who say,
Come on you can trust me?

We're trying to hold some space,
For compassion,
But we're left in the dark,
After the spiral of passion,
Passionately dies,
After we keep on hearing,
Little white lies.

Nobody cares,
If no one's around,
We're lost in the rapture,
Of living in our house or home,
The truth is not something we capture,
Within our Stockholm syndrome,
Making excuse after excuse,
For the unknown.

We just keep going to the back,
Of every queue,
Back to the basics,
Of one plus two.

Verbal Jujitsu

In our quantum field,
What we relinquish,
Is in what we yield,
And in whatever we punish.

Some might say,
That there's another way,
To stop fighting the waves,
As we are the fish,
We are the ocean,
We are awesome in combination.

It's all,
In what we say,
Tempers unravel,
When they begin to fray,
To win any war,
Is to deny the first battle,
Looking from a different angle,
Violence is the lowest form of communication,
When it gets too much for the ego to handle,
How do we defuse each situation?

Every World Champion loses their crown,
So no one achieves,
By bringing somebody down,
It's never a title,
That's full of charisma,
It's that look with a smile,
It's that one vital hug,
That shows how much,
They really miss ya.

Wisdom speaks softly,
With little to prove,
We don't have to confront,
Every confrontation,
With the first move.

The best fight we'll ever have,
Is the one we'll never have,
What once seemed so important,
Developed a favourable fault,
Like an on and off switch,
Has returned to default.

Let animosity go,
It takes two to tango,
In the dance of who is braver,
Do yourself a favour,
Being reasonable,
With someone unreasonable,
Is the real power,
The power of love,
A silver tongue hits harder,
Than a fist in a glove.

There's a valuable lesson,
In de-escalation,
We can't win or lose a war,
That we're not in,
In a cynical world,
There's no right equation,
But we hold the capacity,
To forgive what they believe in.

In whatever we say,
In whatever we do,
What harm would it do,
To practice verbal jujitsu?

Cataclysmic Shift

It's in our own inner voice,
All those voices in our heads,
It's our own choice,
What we choose to dismiss,
After it's been fed.

From the New World Order,
To the World Health Organisation,
Their violations,
Are destined to cause disorder,
Incrementally,
We have been inundated,
Their cryptic coercion,
Subliminally goes on.

Does every man become manipulated,
Like putty thrown,
Into their pantheon,
It's been going on for too long.

Echoes from the chamber cry,
Build back better,
Pardon me,
But what are we,
Building back better from,
We won't lower our vibrations,
Our consciousness will not succumb,
We know what feels wrong,
Bygones need a chance,
To let bygones be bygones.

Third Time Truly Loving Unconditionally

Digging in our heels,
We follow no one,
And we just can't keep on,
Beating ourselves up,
Over what others have done,
By staying within our hearts,
We find the lion's roar for every woebegone.

We're drifting,
As we are set adrift,
We all now play our part,
In this cataclysmic shift,
What sets us apart,
Brings us together,
Listening to our hearts,
With our very own stethoscope,
We don't have to live in horror,
Of somebody else's horror scope.

In our world of hyper scrutiny,
Redefined lurks the price we pay,
In the demise of their fiat currency,
Is our chance to jump ship,
Away from slavery.

Can we give ourselves,
That fundamental change,
You can't change who is around you,
If they're not ready,
After pouring bucket loads of empathy,
Over everyone,
When do we refill with compassion,
We just keep on,
Keeping on,
Until we move on.

Do we need to change who is around us,
Yes we could spend a lifetime,
Discussing the weather,
Whether it's all controlled,
Sunshine or rain,
Some things will never change,
Until we change them,
We always have the chance to think again.

Our fathers foretold this moment,
That's now begun,
That much needed lift,
For every one,
It's the beginning of our twinning,
With our cataclysmic shift.

Afoot

Are we all just coming and going,
Without the slightest possibility,
Of knowing,
What's staged and contrived,
What's secretly happening,
What's afoot?

Everyone should have known better,
Soot falls down a chimney,
When it's disturbed,
Who's heard of candid confusion,
When nobody said a single word,
Ignorance is not a valid excuse,
In this age of information,
What is afoot?

Psyop after psyop,
What's the undercurrent to each disease,
Who's for the chop,
Believing some hypothesis,
Right here right now,
The bubble goes pop,
Bursts so quick
Holy mackerel,
Holy cow,
Holy sees through those who are sick.

Where are the lions roaring,
When we're still exploring,
Chopping down the twisted vines,
Of scare mongering,
Using fear is their biggest trick,
How can our Mother Earth stay healthy,
When the vast majority of humanity,
Are tired,
Are sick?

Who is out there,
Chopping away at our toxicity,
Trying to save us,
From fatality?

Hey there sleepy head,
Have those bells stopped ringing,
Have they stopped advertising,
What's alarming,
What's afoot?

It's time we let go,
Of our Quasimodo,
And put this bed time story,
Back to bed,
History doesn't seem to happen,
Until it's read,
All this painful, spiteful, vengeful hatred.

Does anybody feel normal,
Does anyone feel a new normal coming,
In our history,
What has ever been normal?

We've been given,
Every debrief,
Every tale,
Every twist,
So much living,
Has now been missed,
Normality just doesn't exist,
It's beyond belief,
Shocked,
Locked down,
And casually blocked.

When will it be dawning,
On those that are conforming,
That are immune system protects us,
Season after season,
Year after year,
We're all still standing here,
Our immune system wouldn't attack us,
For no reason.

Looking fearlessly with a loving eye,
What's faked as real,
We don't have to buy,
Our bodies are working over time to heal.

Can't we see from within,
What's becoming blatantly obvious,
After being obviously put,
Don't you now feel,
That something's afoot?

Something's Gotta Give

Fortitude and strength,
Add length,
To the longest list,
Well it's not gonna get,
Any worse than this,
We're going through the biggest crisis,
I told you so,
But nobody wants to be told,
When everybody's a benevolent witness.

As the stars aligned,
Our ancestors and passed loved ones,
Out there in the nebulae,
Were crying out,
'What does your heart say',
Every life lesson,
Won't be messing,
With whatever you're going to do anyway.

We endure courage with adversity,
As everybody is subject,
To their own reality,
There's little leverage,
With the cause and effect,
How quickly we forget.

The fabric of reality could split,
Into another colostomy bag of bullshit,
It's not what we have done,
It's what we are going to do,
Within someone else's simulation,
How do we find a place to fit into?

Mindful,
That we're not there yet,
Within the theatre of our minds,
Their stories have lost the plot,
It's the blind that lead the blind,
It's like there's a pillar box of protection,
With us tugging on the Jenga blocks,
Of deception,
Something's gotta give.

We're extraordinarily scared,
Doing extraordinary things,
How can we express ourselves,
So calmly,
When they're harming you,
They're harming me,
Seizures, blood clots,
Bell's Palsy, fevers,
None of this is ordinary,
Something's gotta give.

Awaken your inner warrior,
We're not insignificant or forgotten,
On a world wide scale,
The stitch has no real suture,
We see everything,
In every little detail,
And just won't take it any more,
We can live,
As we want to live,
And we have a life,
To live for.

Blame Me

Some emotions are only found,
Outside the only,
Upon our loneliest treadmill,
We run scenarios through the mind,
We mill things over,
So many questions left over,
About what we're going through.

Find as you find,
But you can blame me,
If it keeps the peace,
Blame me for being unlikeable,
It's not you,
It's me that's dividable.

This one's for you,
Not every manifestation,
Plays out as it plays,
Or becomes restored,
After being ignored,
After every lion has roared,
We're all cried out,
And haven't slept for days.

So blame me,
For showing as much,
As a closed book,
What part of a loving conversation,
Hits like a bull in a china shop,
Blame me for,
All the things that were never spoken,
All the hearts left broken.

Are you gonna blame me,
For all the things,
I've never said,
But every unspoken word,
Is floundering in love,
Sentimentality in its infancy,
Fundamentally,
I never thought,
This could happen to me.

Sorry is the word that is said,
After it's over,
For the lack of enthusiasm,
That has incurred,
The hardest goodbye ever heard.

But please don't blame me,
For writing a love poem,
For me,
It's the love,
That makes it real,
Love changes everything,
Love's found somewhere,
Outside the loneliness,
Always ready to bless.

It's easy to write a love poem,
And this one's for you,
It goes on filling hearts,
I give it all in parts of thereof,
Love rebuilds the bridges of forgiveness,
That way is love.

From what rose from obscurity,
To somewhere beyond eternity,
Our love grew to coalesce,
For all souls,
That became blameless,
Blame me.

Flame Of A Thought

We are now able,
To do things,
We couldn't before,
Feeling more.

It's undeniable,
That we could never live,
The same moment twice,
We're ready for something bigger,
There's never a bad time,
For a road trip,
To sit around the campfire,
With just a flame of thought,
As our souls testifier.

How can we manifest a future,
When it's all so unpredictable,
When we're consuming chaos,
In our daily debacles.

Everything clashes,
Everything crashes,
There's so much of everything happening,
Fear can deceive,
And can be so convincing,
Get behind us Satan,
There's nowhere left,
For you to spawn.

The foreseeable future flips,
To readjust,
God save us,
From the hypnotic subconscious seduction,
The genocide depopulation,
As the skies turn red,
May we live more inside our hearts,
Than inside our heads,
Within this insurrection,
Of a new dawn.

When will we question,
All we've been taught,
From the spark of an idea,
To the flame of a thought,
Have we forgotten,
What makes us glow,
Bare foot on the grass,
Feeling grounded from head to toe?

How quickly it can all comes to pass,
Ageing so rapidly,
This is getting serious,
Have we been needlessly waiting,
For what unfolds before us?

Is whatever is functional,
Best left alone,
Why do we keep on updating,
The telephone?

You can call me a cynic,
You can call a dreamer,
But opinions are like onions,
With layers that can never concur.

There's still so much happening,
Happening naturally,
Happening spontaneously,
And it doesn't have to be,
Guilt tripped,
Coerced,
Persuaded or reminded.

Our bodies and minds,
Are always detoxing,
Seeking out the body and soul,
Over what's said,
Intuition in living.

The twin flame burns brightly within,
The flame of a thought,
Burns way out of control,
To never give in,
To give the best,
To become more,
Than we thought we could be,
To give it a go,
To live our lives free,
To live our best life,
To be.

Loving Unconditionally

Love and light,
Two and the same,
All that we are,
And in-between,
All that we overcame.

Turning it all inside out,
Outpouring,
Talking to the Universe,
As it's always listening,
Effortless,
In the effort she brings.

Love holds unconditional truth,
To light up the World,
Unexplainable,
Inexplicable and magical,
Our oneness with all.

All is love,
No conditions,
No boundaries,
Self-healing,
Self nurturing,
Within and beyond,
You and me,
Loving unconditionally,
A collective awakening.

Every satanic agenda,
We are resisting,
Unconditionally loving,
One another,
Unwavering is the memory,
That we remember,
That fulfilling feeling,
Of being there for each other.

It's that helping hand,
That holds the tightest,
Where would we be,
If love wasn't a part of this?

Love's the highest frequency,
Love is creation,
Within its own energy,
Empathy,
Turns the soul of plenty.

Self-centred in its own selflessness,
Our internal garden,
Is grown from above,
With gratitude, appreciation and admiration,
You already know,
All possible things are possible,
Beautiful soul,
Loving unconditionally,
You are loved.

The greatest miracle,
That's universal,
Is our connection,
With all living beings,
The light hearted parted,
The sea of divinity,
The blissfulness of things,
In alignment with you,
To yourself be true.

Love's something that's sacred,
Awareness is widespread,
In all that we do,
All that's ahead.

That floaty feeling,
Cartwheeling love mixed with joy,
Everything has every potential,
For us to enjoy,
Blissfully loving,
When we're loving blissfully,
Loving unconditionally.

People Power

Never had much time,
For those with the perceived power,
For their tyranny,
Wrapped up in their pageantry,
The evil satanic freemasonry,
With oaths of secrecy,
Information kept from our society.

The power of the people,
Is much more,
Than the people in power,
Together we are powerful,
Together in arms,
We don't want to bow down any more,
Shoulder to shoulder,
A shield of protection,
In this belligerent battle,
Of good versus evil.

We pray for change,
From the monarchy,
We pray for mercy,
From the hierarchy,
From their system of exploitation,
What good,
What kind of salvation,
Has ever come from war,
What is war for,
Call me naive,
But I believe,
It takes only one man,
To change the World,
To fight no more.

Truth and untruth,
Simultaneously collide,
In a simulation,
Of chest dangling medals,
Worn ceremonially,
In an imitation of pride.

Injustice is found in the mess,
Of another unfounded judgment,
It falls on our shoulders,
To care for a stranger,
Not to put them in danger,
Creating divisions,
Creating divides.

The more that we want something,
The more that we go after it,
But beware of the carrot,
And who's holding it.

We will never give up,
Or give our power away,
To a medley of false idols,
That sees us,
As their prey.

None of us,
Are powerless,
We have the peoples' power potential,
We won't stop the squeeze,
Until every corrupt corporation,
Is brought to its knees.

Third Time Truly Loving Unconditionally

People are power,
We are the people,
The powerful population,
As we join together,
All with the power of our correlation,
Within the peoples' union.

This Ain't About Me

Right now,
At this moment in time,
As you're reading this poem,
How are you doing,
How is it going,
In life's long list of lessons,
Which ones are really bestowing?

In our World,
Where everything,
Just seems to be scanned,
Do we take it all on the chin,
Lie back,
And think of England?

There's no going back,
Here today,
Gone tomorrow,
In a click of our fingers,
Another lifetime has passed,
In our unjust World,
Of where, when and why,
We're always busy earning a crust,
When will our number be up,
When will our passing be nigh?

We know that unconditional love,
Is something that money can't buy,
Fame is not love,
And success is not money,
There's nothing that's materialistic,
That could ever satisfy.

This ain't about me,
Trying to fill a chasm so vast,
No one can stop what's coming,
You'll see,
When we all stand aghast.

The great awakening,
Is within,
What begins today,
Truly begins,
Woe betide the price we pay,
We won't be in a world of suffering,
If we don't see it that way.

Inside every misapprehension,
Is a moment in which we're lacking,
We are not just acquaintances,
Never to be acquainted,
Always attacking,
We have all travelled through the madness,
Into our collage of togetherness.

This ain't about me,
When it's all about us,
Self preservation won't make anyone victorious,
We're not in a one man band,
We're living and breathing the same air,
No man is an island,
There's enough of everything to go around,
When we want to share.

In our life's portrait,
In our fantasising,
We are never alone,
Maybe it takes a lifetime of portraying,
Before we find our way home,
Maybe it's all mapped out,
Inside of you,
From the beginning?

So before you logout and disappear,
Here's a little something,
I think you always knew,
You don't have to seek out,
The World's most qualified practitioner,
Because that practitioner,
Has always been you.

It's All Coming Back

There are those artefacts,
That decompose,
Or are shaped into being,
Like a sprinkle of sawdust,
Shifting sands are garnishing,
What's left behind,
There's no random acts,
Everything's connected,
Corrected,
Taking up all the slack,
It's all coming back.

Nothing's coincidental,
The turning tides are incremental,
In going forward,
And in reversal,
Akin to what's happening,
Our guides move through out,
The realms of the spiritual.

All those old ways of being,
Are how we become,
Who we've always been,
We go therein to herein,
To feel our elegiac feelings.

On the path of ascending,
The cycles have shifted,
We see that we're inherently gifted,
Like a veil has been lifted,
From the slings and arrows,
Of yesterday's sorrows.

It's a brand new day,
With a brand new way,
Of doing things,
Everything's bursting into life,
With this new found energy within,
Everything's erupted,
With the excitement of everything,
Wrapped up in love's oldest anorak,
So much of something,
Has something to show,
It's all coming back.

Embracing a world,
That was once forgotten,
As we leave the spectrum,
To make something happen,
We'll never think of ourselves,
In the same way again,
The old love's coming back again.

It's begun and it's here,
The peace of a thousand years,
The sovereign has let go,
Of our souvenirs.

From our sacrum,
To our cerebrum,
We'll be taken aback,
What a time to be alive,
It all has arrived,
What's in front of us,
Is in front of us now,
It's all coming back.

Parroting

Somewhere between,
There's just an empty space,
Even after every emotion,
Gets another promotion.

Conversation collateral,
Isn't so natural,
As we don't think,
Of all this alone,
Anything is anything,
To a revelation,
Setting a scene,
All the World's a stage,
As we engage,
In what we believe,
Will make us happy,
Why can't we,
Stop acting naively,
And simply act more naturally?

Is anybody being original,
While we're casting off our confidence,
Patience holds out for pretence,
In the depths of acceptance,
While we're keeping our distance.

Cheerfully chirping cheerio,
Keeping up the illusion of the status quo,
Without a mustard seed of faith,
Repeating what's appropriate,
Like the parrot to the pirate,
With nowhere to go.

Therein lies the entrapment,
Of the parrot,
Living without thinking,
Drawing a blank,
It's madness,
Willingly walking the plank.

When the majority are parroting fear,
Does anybody ever comprehend,
What's manifesting,
Ready to appear,
We don't have to let our hearts,
Fill with so much pain,
When will it end,
If there's no way out of here?

When will we,
Let it be,
We are valuable,
Not vulnerable,
Healthy mind,
Healthy body.

When will we question personal gain,
Life is futuristically unfolding,
Now there's no denying,
That the green eyed monster,
Has lost her reign,
After every overlord,
Has gone overboard,
Creating sadness with honour.

When will we just be ourselves,
Approving ourselves,
Without approval,
Are we lost within the trauma,
Of drama?

We can't just hide away,
Praying for a better day,
While trapped within this scenario,
Bending the truth through,
The positions of prisms,
Has what's occurred,
Somehow blurred our visions?

Today's the day,
For us to start again,
Without setting the scene,
Moving away,
From where we have been,
Being ourselves,
Without all that parroting.

Here

Could of written a love poem,
Let go,
To fall in love,
Could of skated on thin ice,
Without falling,
From above.

Could of watched the stars,
Without a pain,
Inside my neck,
Could of won the lottery,
But that's not an ability,
So what the heck?

Could of held your hand,
Even though my palms were sweaty,
Could of changed the World,
If my imagination had shown me.

Could of sang your song,
If it wasn't for embarrassment,
Could have lived so long,
If it wasn't for attachment.

Could of been a good day,
If good had been on my mind,
Could of helped out more,
Breaking boundaries,
Being kind.

Could of asked more questions,
But the silence grew,
Could of made more spontaneous mistakes,
Right out of the blue.

Could of lead the way,
Been a living inspiration,
Could of shared much more,
Than just scenarios of each situation.

Could of lived in nature,
Instead of inside some box,
Could of practised yoga,
Released those arthritic knots.

Could of worn a smile,
Instead of a complicated frown,
Could of read more books,
The words were always written down.

Could of taken far more risks,
The stakes were never high,
Could of watched the sun rise,
From the horizon to the sky.

Could of really lived my life,
Until the day I died,
Could have done so much,
If it wasn't for the fear,
For fear was life's greatest illusion,
Of a sickness,
That was never here.

Ripples In The Ether

In our intuitive journey,
We're forever worthy,
And we don't know how lucky,
We are,
On our spiritual journey,
Within our physical body,
We have walked on the waters,
To come ashore,
And we don't know how far we've come,
But we have travelled so far,
On our heartfelt journey.

All those moments we forever keep,
Every night we smiled,
Ourselves to sleep,
All those light hearted lifts,
All those imaginative gifts,
And still we don't know,
Still waters run deep.

How powerful we are,
We are the light,
Behind the energy,
We will,
Love you still,
As we ripple through the ether,
Having our best day ever,
Eternal inside our eternity.

We can do incredible things,
Shifts and transformations,
Life's manifestations,
Life's greatest blessings.

Everything's alive,
Either within a state of becoming,
Or a state of decaying,
What is it that we're creating,
When we are ageing?

In the ever present,
We are what we choose,
Behind all alchemy of magic,
We never stay the same,
While living inside the now,
Between the tragical and fantastical,
Somewhere in the ether,
Our daily autobiography,
Reads with a wow.

Mindful with motivation,
Inspirational with inspiration,
In love,
With association,
The day we leave this material plane,
We fly with wings,
To our terrain,
Sending ripples into the ether,
No longer separated,
No longer discombobulated,
By never the twain.

Something Wonderful

We're beginning to wonder,
What's going to materialise,
From the words we analyse,
Maximise,
Within the maxim of joinder,
Curiouser and curiouser,
Authenticity has been lost within hypocrisy,
Catching us by surprise.

The Queen has played her game,
Ripping us to shreds,
Just like all those arrowheads,
That are so heavily fixed,
The outcome comes out the same,
It's off with our heads,
Otherwise who else is to blame,
The rabbit holes always been there,
It's just under a new name.

Running along with the rabbits,
Retaining bad habits,
Always on the hop,
With no time to stop,
We're all for the chop.

Kaloo,
Kalay,
Now let's not delay,
From escaping the inevitable,
There's no running away,
The Mad Hatter and the Hare,
Are having an unbirthday somewhere,
Now what does that really say?

Everyone who is here,
Is crazy and weird,
What time is it,
Who's got the time,
As soon as it's here,
Time's disappeared,
It's something that we'll never own,
But it's made so easily,
For all and sundry,
Don't you believe me?

There's no limitations,
That we are living under,
But before we can see it,
We've got to believe it,
Your dreams and dedication,
Are such a wonderful combination,
What appears at your pleasure,
Are in the moments you treasure.

Together we're gamely growing,
Into tomorrow,
Without really knowing,
Gliding into something so graceful,
Into something so wonderful.

Dream big,
Or don't dream at all,
Do you really wonder or think,
Because now I think,
That's your call.

Unrequited Love

If we're looking for the point,
Of love,
It's at that point,
We move away,
So far,
From what we're looking for,
There's no rhyme or reason,
For our hearts to carry scars.

We're our own interpretations,
Of someone,
Somewhere in the future,
We carry so many expectations,
With so many successions of emotions,
Why do we expect,
So many uninvited saviours?

Yes we're all connected,
But maybe we're neglected,
For the premise of something better,
Going through the motions of existence,
We just can't drag hope around,
Like a debt collector,
Kicking and screaming with persistence.

No one,
Owes a life long debt to another,
Every single one of ya,
It's not a game of what comes back,
When it's out there in the ether.

When it hits,
It hits right out of the park,
A sparks a spark,
Igniting flames of desire,
To warm the cockles,
Of our connected hearts.

Is there any complete certainty,
In the ceremony,
Of once you know,
You know,
Love takes everything so damn personally,
When love involves,
The psychological trappings of the ego,
Every circumstance,
Creates a chance,
To let love's light really glow.

All the opinions and assumptions,
Load the pointed gun of someone's fate,
Can we ever have a different view,
Without the baggage of so much weight?

Within each sublime moment we lose time,
Butterflies are all aflutter,
When we're reunited,
We're so excited,
As we mutter,
I love you,
To each other.

In anticipation of what's ahead,
Let's all go softly as we tread,
Unrequited love,
Does it really matter,
No,
Not if we love ourselves,
Instead.

Where Do We Go?

Where do we go,
When it's all down on paper,
Our word is our deed,
But sooner or later,
We only answer to our creator,
Keep faith and pray,
We don't need,
A mediator,
If we've lost our way.

After each meeting of minds,
Humanity has its long list,
Of crimes,
Who acts as a person,
Who acts as a corporation,
Have we been sold down the river,
Being registered,
As a placenta,
We came into being,
Weighed as an amateur.

Living man,
Living woman,
We all arrived first,
In our delivery,
Why do we travel along,
With this tomfoolery,
Was that our first mistake,
In our fraudulent history?

On the day of our birth,
Why were we not aware,
That we were born,
Does sea monster mean human,
They've been lying to us from day one,
Every morning,
We no longer mourn.

The weekend,
Has the majority weakened,
As we sing happy birthday,
It's not for some,
Really,
Come on,
We're not a ship coming into port,
Or lost at sea,
Waiting to be caught.

Who is it that we're really afraid of,
What is it,
That we factually know,
I'm a man,
Doing all that I can,
To rewrite the confusion,
Where do we go,
Into the mind,
Into the soul,
With the honesty of our indwelling spirit,
With straight forwardness and integrity,
What we know with certainty,
We know with clarity.

Do we now get it,
Is it all just an act,
Do we all prefer the hypothetical,
A false pretender,
Will call all and sender,
A hypocrite,
The aristocrats live in their ivory towers,
Do we as a collective concur,
That all this is counterfeit,
Fake money and powers?

To change the fabric of society,
Lets start at the beginning,
Our birth certificate,
They call it official,
But does a copy of a copy,
Make anything real,
We were all born,
Born real.

As a soul,
We've been capitalised on since that first day,
As every signed document,
Is under containment,
Of the four corner rule,
We're nobodies fool,
As this severance of trust,
Is so unjust,
For one and all,
Where do we go?

Beggars Belief

It's a different point of view,
Inside a different ball game,
It doesn't really happen,
Right out of the blue,
As we're subjected to,
All the Government's mind games.

It's the misguided few,
That somehow believe the old cliché,
That they're pulling the strings,
Their misuse of perceived power,
Brings whatever it brings,
Gaslighting while filibustering,
Seducing to increase wanting,
To divide us apart,
Their characteristics are sour,
As they never,
Have our best interests at heart.

The mind boggles,
At all their dogma and rules,
Does anybody legitimately care,
Why are so many unaware,
Of the Covidian psychosis,
We can't just keep going along,
With reliance and compliance,
To this,
When it all seems so morally wrong,
We can reason with reason,
But come on everyone,
Isn't it about time we begin,
To reason with cognition?

We are all equals,
Within our equilibrium,
We're all connected,
With both the Earth and the animal kingdom,
Evolution evolves,
With each distribution.

When will we become,
All that we are,
To be the corroborative,
To live and let live,
When will we all become anti-war?

Life's a loaded gun,
It's so full of objectives,
As we're so fired up,
With the long list of directives,
But we're always the first soul,
That we have to get on with,
As we learn to love ourselves,
We learn to treat others,
How we would like to be treated.

Okay so there are multiple minds,
Coming from different perspectives,
Each day we find as we find,
As human kind has defined,
Each and every man made storm,
Every time the politicians,
Ask us to conform,
It's like wearing a mask,
That's laced with chloroform.

Third Time Truly Loving Unconditionally

There's circumstances and conditions,
That we should all live by,
But it beggars belief,
Why we don't now comply,
To all of us doing no harm?

Hope
(In Our Choosing)

We can and we do,
Accomplish whatever is our task,
Each time we ask,
For help along our journey,
As we unravel,
We travel,
And hope helps to make,
Our burdens easier to carry.

The ever eternal optimist,
Never once missed,
Each and every catastrophe,
But the optimist knew,
That with God's love and some hope,
They'll be able to cope,
And always pull through.

What's happening now,
Will not last forever,
Even though now,
Is always here in every endeavour,
If we hang onto hope,
Then by design,
We never resign.

If you were to write three words,
To post to yourself in an envelope,
What would they be,
Words full of encouragement to the addressee?

If you were to look,
Through the eye of a telescope,
What in the world,
Would you want to see,
A world full of wonderment and malleability?

Hope is the beginning of an idea,
We're looking at the bigger picture here,
Finding ourselves out there,
So abundant in scope,
Hope's springing up in everything everywhere,
Listen to those birds,
Day after day they sing,
Forever healing our cosmic energy,
Uplifting us,
Bringing hope,
With their dawn chorus.

Hope is all around us,
Going on uncharted adventures,
Of uncharted discovery,
Go out and hug a tree,
Swim in the deep sea,
There's nothing that's impossible,
Nothing you can't do,
Hope you'll find something,
That works for you.

Right here,
Right now,
You're in the right place,
There's no other time,
Like right now,
It's always the now we have to face.

Taking it one step at a time,
It's your time to shine,
Hope's your preparation,
For the very next climb.

We are all in this together,
Every sister and brother,
Our secret to happiness,
Is to help one another,
And after you've read this poem,
Right now today,
Hope you know that you're stronger,
Than any challenge,
That comes your way.

Whether your winning, drawing or losing,
You've got this,
You do,
With a pocket full of hope,
There for your choosing,
To carry you through.

Discombobulated

We're travelling within the spectrums,
Of all those indistinguishable locations,
Have we lost our way,
In the price we pay,
Are we slaves to the system,
Until we no longer buy the lies,
From the liars that tell them?

In an unnatural world,
Where the ego plays at being a friend,
We have swallowed so much pride,
Hiding within the shadows of generalisation,
Are we courageous enough to wipe the slate clean,
After observing from a long life of observation,
That we are not liberated,
If we are obligated.

Discombobulated,
While drunk within the sobriety of grieving,
Trying to process the sanity,
As we experience the experience,
Leaving us shattered,
But now we're shattering illusions,
It's absurd to live,
This stereotyped farce,
Of ignorance is bliss,
Because the reality is harsh.

Action and consequence,
Are building the foundation,
Of what we believe to be true,
After everything we thought we knew,
Was an excruciating lie,
Ascending we wave goodbye,
Awakening to awareness,
In our ever evolving transition.

Anything is doable,
When everything is shown,
The future is unconditional,
Until the future is foreknown.

To predict the future,
Is to use anything and everything,
To create it,
As we take on every system,
We put a spanner in the works,
To break it.

The calibre of one's character,
Has grown from the ashes,
From life's lemon that they squeeze,
From the apprentice to our own trustee,
From the trappings of the high trapeze,
We have to let it go.

The whole House of Commons collapses,
When who's being governed,
Becomes ungovernable,
Money has been used to tax us into slavery,
We have to become responsible,
Extinguishing conformity,
With our heartfelt morality.

There'll be an explosion of excitement,
There'll be a flood of pure enlightenment,
As we grow into our sovereignty,
As we deal with our own genie.

The message in a bottle,
Will make the common denominator topple,
Unravelling all those discombobulated threads,
Like wild fire it all spreads,
Until it begins to melt,
We stand unbroken,
From being discombobulated we have awoken,
Because everything was intuitively felt.

The Worldly Way

One way or another,
Leads to the worldly way,
Free from the shackles of society,
Free from the long deviaty,
Of those parasitical globalists,
The Establishment's rule book,
Has been ripped up,
All those demanding lists.

We all have this great ability,
To challenge everything that we know,
As we throw,
A curve ball of susceptibility,
At their creation for destruction show.

The truth is far stranger than fiction,
At no point,
Is their point perfectly proven,
Do we now deny every shroud of evidence,
As the crusade of common sense,
Comes into fruition?

Nothing shall remain hidden,
Nothing shall dwell in secrecy,
The darkness is now exposed,
For the whole World to see.

We are not our past beliefs,
Living by what we are told,
In an unfulfilled calling,
Our time is no longer sold,
The fruits of our labour,
Don't require earning a living,
We are alive,
Already living.

From the disillusionment of different people,
To the whole kit and caboodle,
The World is not ending,
As God is always watching,
The World is upgrading,
Here for the duration,
Creation is love,
And love is creation.

Who needs a referral,
To what's clairvoyantly seen,
As we're reborn,
From a perpetual has been?

We're all energy in spirit,
On our human journey,
We have more in common,
Than could ever divide us,
There's always another way,
That's not always obvious,
A way with more opportunity,
Liberty, solidarity and posterity.

From the intelligent,
To the intellectual,
From the superficial,
To the spiritual,
We are all glorious,
In unconditional love,
The stratosphere,
Expands here,
Right before us,
Below just as above.

It's the worldly way,
Even though,
Some wordly words can warily weigh,
We don't have to be,
Susceptible to suggestion,
As we know,
We can't change the facts,
Only our feelings towards them.

Precipitated Panic

Is everything fine,
Oh no,
Not this time,
What's going on here,
As terror tears right through,
The atmosphere?

Are we being coerced,
Towards another rehearsed calamity,
Of mores the pity,
When we still feel,
That something is missing,
Can we smell a rat,
God meet us,
At the place where we're at.

In contradiction with ourselves,
As we try to flee,
But within our capacity,
All things can happen,
Synchronicity will mindfully,
Come randomly,
Patience puts trust in the process,
Nothing more,
Nothing less.

We will never be,
The same again,
The day we release,
The greatest thief,
Comparison,
How can we resolve,
The web that we wove,
If joy is left in incarceration?

After every outcome,
That we accommodate,
Every action in which we participate,
After every precipitated panic,
That we anticipate,
Who is being authentic?

Why are we surrounded by lies,
When its the truth that never dies,
With a figment of our imagination,
Can we look the world straight in the eye,
And question,
Where's our obligation,
To kneel down,
To the malfeasance acts,
Of those bully boy,
And their belligerent acts,
Of terrorism?

There's no formal agreement,
We have not agreed to be governed,
By paper shufflers,
In a paper secret society,
No one walking this Earth,
Has any authority,
Over another.

We don't need dependency,
The Government has no authority,
Over us,
The police have no authority,
Over us,
The judges have no authority,
Over us.

It's like we have over indulged,
On wasabi peas,
Bringing us to our knees,
What we digest becomes part of our being,
Living in some precipitated panic,
Without any meaning.

In layman's terms,
If a man lays down,
Expect to be walked on,
Now know thyself,
Know that your awesome.

Helping A Stranger

We all start off as strangers,
On life's conveyor belt of emotions,
Snowballing the debris of our past,
Wrapped up in childhood trauma,
And ancestral trauma,
That just wants to last,
Vulnerability doesn't hold the catalyst to danger,
The dam will burst if we hold it all inside,
Damn it,
If you're mad,
Get mad.

How can outside influences,
Ever be our true saviour,
Salt and sugar,
Can kill in equal measure,
So let's break bread together,
Everybody is born an amateur,
In helping a stranger.

It wasn't about me,
It never really was,
As I reveal,
Each one of my flaws,
I don't want approval,
Or any applause,
If I'm doing good,
I just do,
Without a reason,
Without a cause,
It's the greatest part of me,
That always rings true.

Everybody lies,
Behind deceit,
When somebody cries,
You make me complete,
The sobering thought,
Is in that convulsive sob,
To most help a stranger,
Is an inside job.

Who does a favour without any fuss,
To gently nudge someone,
Out of the way,
Of an oncoming bus?

When we don't listen to anybody,
Don't feed the hungry,
Or talk to the lonely,
If we don't help a stranger,
It'll become a tragedy,
If we don't help each other collectively,
Let's not all become addicted,
To our own personal safety.

What's life any way,
Without a coin toss,
We've got to take our chances,
Without being restricted,
When will we build bridges,
For our hearts to cross,
After we've had so much absence,
After we've had so much loss.

We do it to ourselves,
When we do battle with ourselves,
The walls of self-preservation,
Build the castles of our incarceration.

Some say,
What's meant to be,
Is meant to be,
But we can't just hide away,
As the wheels of destruction keep turning,
The shoulder of blame,
Should be on thee,
If we're not showing courage,
In the face of adversity,
If we're not putting aside our differences,
For all of humanity,
A stranger is a friend,
That's yet to be.

Sweet Fanny Adams

Every illusion,
Is now escaping perception,
Leading to just another misconception,
We always knew,
There's nothing but a perceptual view,
That's past the horizon.

It's like everything unfathomable is lost,
Even the horizon is not real,
There's nothing left of any consequence,
That's tangible to feel,
Making no sense,
Feeling bereft,
Dripping in synthetic sweat,
Do we even know what is real any more,
Where is the honesty,
Fairness and decency,
To fill our hearts up with integrity?

Why do we do,
All that we do,
And who is it for,
Our seeds cannot grow,
If there is nowhere to plough,
So we can't allow
The day to arrive,
When we are so deprived
Doing are worst,
Within some kind of meta universe,
Immersed and consumed,
In a place where we're doomed,
Dying to survive.

We're facing daily controversy,
How far will we let,
This soul destroying spiritual war,
Carry on for,
After years and years of suffering,
We beat our chests,
Letting our lion hearts roar,
Those that are oppressed,
We can no longer ignore.

We're all too instinctual,
To ever fall,
For the rich man's tricks,
After the money has gone,
We'll do right over wrong,
After every millionaire to billionaire,
Disappears quick,
Then we will see for ourselves,
Who is left to care,
Just by being there.

Like a dog running around,
Chasing its tail,
The whole monetary system,
Is bound to fail,
The buck stops with us,
We can come up with a million excuses,
But the web of lies,
Either widens or reduces.

We've had a gut full of lies,
We're left with the collateral remains,
After what's fictional,
Where are the facts,
That were forsworn,
We're not sacrificial lambs,
Being pulled over the edge,
As useless eaters,
Our conscience has not under gone,
Its own dementia.

It's a two way street,
And sometimes we can see,
Ourselves coming,
From a place,
Where we've once been,
That was so unbecoming.

Are we gradually losing ourselves,
To identity theft,
Till there's hardly a trace of us left,
From the day we were born,
Just like poor sweet Fanny Adams,
Our hearts,
Are now torn,
Every day that we mourn.

Lambs To The Slaughter

The lamb in all its divine calm,
Is calling out,
Over the ills of this World,
To do no harm,
To do no more harm.

The lamb without a blemish,
Is crossing the equator,
We are shining upon our Mount Sinus,
As all the saints,
Go marching in,
The calculator has lost count,
Of all that amounts,
All that lays before us.

It all has to be seen,
As it is seen,
The navigating lights,
Are as bright as they've ever been,
The stars are the maps,
Of magnetism,
Shining on snowflakes,
Divine intervention,
In unison.

All the resurrections,
All the shifts and ascensions,
All the mysteries will occur,
The wolves won't come a knocking,
They won't come to your door,
We're always detoxing what isn't pure,
There's no cure for the common cold,
Because the common cold is the cure.

Third Time Truly Loving Unconditionally

We all rise above,
And we do this together,
Love is no feat,
As we tread the superstition,
Of our conviction,
Away from defeat.

We rise above,
To walk upon the maritime waters,
We rise from our crawl,
Above it all,
With the power of love,
Almighty love,
We are no longer,
Lambs to the slaughter,
We are responsible for everything,
There is so much we can alter.

Those were the days,
As these are the days,
The theology of philosophy,
That no one picks-up,
Beliefs fall like Autumn leaves,
When technology shuts up.

Jerusalem,
Has lost its enthusiasm,
Built up over centuries,
The light has grown stronger,
Like a lightbulb exploding,
In all its euphoric eruption,
We're no longer unaware,
Of all the corruption.

We're only now,
Just getting started,
Collectively getting away,
From what's been distorted.

Away,
From all their predispose methods,
That they've always taught ya,
Away,
From their manipulative manifesto frauds,
Away,
From being in front of the firing squads,
Away,
From being lambs to the slaughter.

Flesh On A Skeleton

We are so much more,
Much, much more than,
Flesh on a skeleton,
We're all equal under the law,
We're a force to be reckoned with,
As nobody is above the law.

We live as we live,
The proof of life,
Is more than just flesh,
Every crèche,
Creates its own crèche,
The truth is simple,
Experience everything that life has to give.

As we are beckoned,
We break up with what's normal,
Our bodies are magical,
Our temples,
Our words are sanctus,
And when we work for energies,
They work for us.

We are the clause,
We are the people,
We are so much more,
Much more than,
Lost souls fallen from Heaven,
We keep the peace,
From a different dimension,
Connecting Adam back to Eve,
Were we ever lost,
Did we ever leave?

We are about to take down everything,
No one can force,
Their will upon you,
No one can tell you what to do.

We dance along with the frequencies,
We are so much above,
As we are beneath,
Every humble opinion,
Every humble belief,
Our thoughts and feelings,
Move out of the mind,
Into the heart,
Worldwide our ripples spawn.

A star in every circumstance,
Expressing our love,
We are shining bright,
Sovereignty invites infinite possibility,
We hold the most,
Beautiful guiding light.

We are so universal,
The best of the best,
A colossal collaboration,
The freedom of obligation,
Of all that has been,
And yet to be,
And all that is past,
And all that is the rest.

Third Time Truly Loving Unconditionally

Feeling a warm vibrant energy,
With every breath of release,
As we raise the vibration,
Co-workers,
Light workers,
We will not breach the peace.

Making a change,
We open the door,
For a better tomorrow,
While using the tongue,
Knowledge can be spoken,
We are so much more,
Than flesh on a skeleton.

Incomparable

Incarnated into different worlds,
Our souls are protected,
By our ancestors,
And never neglected,
By our higher selves,
Each soul is incomparable,
Not reimbursable.

For those that do not die,
Within the vastness of the Universe,
The battle is within you,
You are beautiful,
That nobody can deny.

Nothing changes,
Without changed behaviour,
No one has ever been born,
Inferior or superior.

We can go through life,
Forever thriving,
Or eternally striving
Our journey is unique,
Though the direction may be the same,
We share this time together,
Even though our characteristics,
Are doing the driving.

We may see the World differently,
Cosmic codes dial through the Torus field,
Towards me,
Challenging what I know,
The Universe is toroidal,
As above,
So below.

From the highest angelic beings,
To the first beings,
In existence,
Creation is custodial,
Architectural by design,
Of subsistence,
Beyond comparison,
Perceptions are rarely withdrawn.

We are all here to share,
Not to leave it there,
Aware as much,
As we are aware.

The truth has never failed to amaze,
Everything is a lie,
Science is a lie,
History is a lie,
In all its complicated simplicity,
We find infinity.

We begin again,
As we began,
Stardust wrapped up within,
Another skin,
Wide awake on the Sea of Tranquillity,
We create our reality,
Exploring each possibility.

They say that we live and learn,
We're the creation of what we imagine,
Now it's your turn,
Stirring the pot of life's casserole,
Whatever we see as sufficient,
Will sufficiently suffice,
Don't sacrifice yourself for the role,
That you play,
You'll have your day,
And that day is today.

Doing your best,
Being your best,
Each and every one of us is able,
Each and every one of us,
Is incomparable.

Signature

New beginnings,
New solutions by solutionists,
There isn't any right way or wrong way,
Of doing things,
There's just different ways,
To put words into the Worldly World,
To say what we mean,
And mean what we say.

We don't need a written contract,
In a contractual paper chase,
Of everything fictional,
Let's get real,
When there's a way,
There's a will.

What pathway we choose,
Leads to whom we become,
Living things,
Anthropoids of Atum,
Even if we are living in a box,
Null and void of the deception,
Each fool's made a fool,
Of the four corner rule,
When making assumptions.

From compliance to authoritarianism,
No one has signed up for this,
From chemical pathogens,
To bio weapons,
We weep at the shots being fired from this,
Can anyone,
Save anyone?

Not all similarities are the same,
Devoid of living,
Unforgiving,
Thrown somewhere into the abyss,
On the day of our birth,
We lost our worth.

The ship has sailed,
Until we sail our own ship,
There's a truth in what we say,
When we're in a rush,
To sign our lives away,
Our signature,
Is our sin in nature.

Our spirit keeps fighting,
The journeyman is on a journey of forgiving,
Through the realms of possibility,
Akin with what we are akin,
Whatever we put into the Universe,
Comes back to us.

In every sign,
Whatever we sign,
We now autograph,
There isn't a signature upon our epitaph,
What's read is red,
Time after time,
It's time to put the bogeyman,
Back to bed.

Third Time Truly Loving Unconditionally

Unconditional love,
Comes without a signature,
True and pure,
To be sure,
To be sure,
To be sure,
It's time to tear up the signature.

Construct Of Time

What is it,
In the name of Gaia,
What is it,
That we're all waiting for,
When is the right time to be right,
Where is our desire for a deeper understanding,
Of our purpose,
In the Universe?

We're standing on the shoulders of giants,
Between the architect of the Universe,
And whatever we conspire,
Every angel has an angle,
As each moment transpires.

Our persistence with patterns,
Our obsession with twenty-four,
Clocking on,
And clocking off,
With all that was before,
Going around in circles,
When is enough,
Enough,
We say,
As we greedily scoff.

How can just surviving,
Be all we're meant to do,
When we walk amongst the starving,
Without responding,
Couldn't we help them through?

Different strokes,
For different folks,
Yes,
That's ignorance indeed,
What is it that we're doing,
If we're not conscious,
Of the ones in need?

Time moves in one direction,
Intriguing within its own disguise,
Observing without judgment,
Until the judgment day arrives,
Schedule after schedule,
Sunset to sunrise,
Between the fourth and fifth dimensions,
Our origin,
It cries,
Where do we now begin?

Spontaneously and naturally,
Time signs its gnarly signature,
For ageing time has no cure,
As one thing follows the other,
Time has thrown away the calendar,
Within the entanglement of time,
We refer,
To what we now refer.

The limits are now limitless,
Paralysed somewhere inside the infinite,
Is an infinite amount of time,
We're all potentially blessed,
As all realities have now progressed,
Way beyond our time,
Consciously foregoing,
Along with the rest,
Simultaneously in time,
God bless.

Hypothetical Meteorite

Nobody knows that they're in a cult,
Until they try to leave it,
Everything we know,
Is what someone else has taught,
Until we feel it.

Riddle me this,
Riddle me that,
We didn't just come here to play a game,
Riddled with obfuscation,
We came here to change it,
To make alterations,
To the established authorities,
And their psychological manipulation,
Indoctrination,
Is indoctrination.

It's biblical,
Or is it biblical deception,
Who hands out letters,
Of religious exemption,
The soul seeks rejuvenation,
The gauntlet's been thrown,
Just as we yearn to have company,
We yearn to be alone.

Reawakening one's mind,
Bringing the mind back to remembrance,
Born through the waters,
Each time they break,
Neither the first step,
Nor the last step,
Are of greater significance,
We're here to take a chance,
For Heaven's sake.

The ego,
Doesn't let go,
Once in the cyclone of unhealed trauma,
We're infinite beings of love,
Pulling the splinter out of our cancel culture,
The truth won't move out of the way,
Of changed behaviour.

We don't have to keep justifying ourselves,
To those who don't care,
We don't have to keep on complying,
To systems that just ain't fair.

On our emotional roller coaster,
Something seems broke,
Smoke and mirrors,
Hide what's been conjured up,
Behind mirrors of smoke.

Who has ever spoken,
Of what makes more sense,
Patience before diligence,
Or diligence before patience,
The karmic fuse is smouldering,
With the weight of this World,
We're shouldering,
The weight of our tolerance,
Our boundaries are the diaries,
Of our reoccurrence.

We've been lying,
To ourselves too much,
Within the Worldly World,
We've been losing touch.

Will we get to thinking,
That something ain't right,
When we are blinking,
At the sky at night,
Trying to catch a glimpse,
Of every hypothetical meteorite?

Walking With You

Has the chord struck a note,
After being played like a fiddle,
We're never given more,
Than we can handle,
Might begets might,
God is with you,
Within the theatre of the human psyche,
Together,
Betrothed in our plight.

Through limitless power,
We promote limitless energy,
What we seek,
Is all around us,
The meek,
Will be,
Aware of human wakefulness,
Put perceptions to the test.

The spirit rises,
Carrying on,
God is with you,
Walking amongst you,
The light doesn't fade,
After every phenomenon.

It's the little things,
That never cease,
As we play with the abundance,
Of a moments peace,
It all requires participation,
Reconnection to reassurance.

It all just begins again,
Time has somehow forgotten the hour,
You can't fight fire with fire,
Don't be discouraged,
When water turns back to vapour,
Lightening doesn't fail,
When it rises back to the creator,
Purpose poses for movement,
Within a glass realm,
Below the firmament.

We will get to do it all,
We feel whatever we feel,
We once played,
In the pouring rain,
Within the esoteric mysteries of the cosmos,
We found love thereof,
Without ever asking,
Grand rising my love,
We're soaring souls shining.

Search your heart,
Within the spiritual milieu,
Take a good look around,
Who's there ready to catch you,
Reaching out a hand,
Who throws a life line,
Shows up with the jump leads,
Of synchronicity,
As we're homeward bound,
All will be fine.

Faith attracts faith,
With the abundance of energy,
Just believe that this is true,
When you're beside yourself,
God is walking with you.

Hero

Our hero,
Distinguished before compassion,
Had perished,
For exceptional courage,
A defender of truth and freedom,
He travelled far from the maddening crowd,
After pondering over the insanity,
Of what's been allowed.

Harmful exposures to misinformation,
Riding on a bus to nowhere,
Trying to get from district to district,
That over night quickly appears,
Our hero will challenge fear,
Our hero,
Is he who says no.

Going it alone,
There'll be no adjournment,
In his discernment,
No inscription is ever needed,
On his journey,
He's never pleaded,
Or had to prove his worth,
Barefoot on this earth,
He cries,
What is war for,
Money, power and greed,
How many souls have to leave,
And who keeps score?

Behind the rage,
He proceeded,
Without an order needed,
Our hero,
Is he who says no,
He says no,
To the mindless destruction,
And death,
To his very last breath.

Our hero,
Is she who says no,
No to the fairy tales,
That have been sold to her,
The pretence of the Prince,
She hasn't been the same since,
She saw the deception of Disney.

On a path not for the faint hearted,
Filled with defiance,
On the day that she started,
Far from the trappings of media compliance,
True to her own sentiments,
Our hero,
Is she who says no.

The end is not the ending,
It's just another reminder,
Of another beginning,
Lest we forget,
God will be watching,
Our hero won't let,
The Worldly World create suffering.

Not all heroes wear capes,
It's our hero who scrapes,
On the wall of illusion,
Until it comes tumbling down,
The mightier they are,
The mightier they fall,
The humblest are blessed,
Not to follow,
Authorities call,
Where's the true obligation,
After all?

The hero,
Our true heroes,
Will stand up,
And not feed the beast,
They will call out,
What is corrupt,
Save so many souls,
From becoming deceased,
They will denounce,
The diabolical demons,
Stop them being released,
For our hero knows,
The power is bestowed,
On the ones,
That sincerely say no.

Boards Of Brilliance

Boards held aloft,
In weathered hands,
With kind regards,
Rebutting carbon cutting plans,
Regarding the future of the unaware hordes,
The fact is we are the carbon,
It's population control,
They're moving towards.

Other notions may get blown,
Right out of the water,
It's depopulation control,
From another dictator.

The masses won't swallow,
Implausible narratives,
After predictive programming,
Never forgives,
With contradiction,
After contradiction,
Let's not wait,
Till tomorrow,
The very next move is up to you,
This ends when we say no.

We become tangled and caught,
Without an original thought,
Caught up in the nothingness,
God bless,
The ones,
With an original feeling,
The schemers are scheming,
In life's game of chess.

The big guns have gone,
Now that the Queen is dead,
After being royally screwed,
It couldn't get any worse,
Being aimlessly lead.

The narrative of events,
Play out like a nail biting whodunnit,
There's no true explanation,
There's no morality behind it.

Whatever unfolds,
Will not become re-foldable,
What's meant to happen,
Was always meant to happen,
Whether or not,
We go to sleep on an argument.

Just when you thought you've heard it all,
Cruel science,
Although it is none the wiser,
Says 'Have a shot of tranquillizer',
It'll never say sorry,
Take it from me.

Don't go along with something,
That makes no sense,
Don't pay the reaper,
His recompense,
Take hold of your life,
Make it the best story ever,
Nobody can live,
Any better.

Third Time Truly Loving Unconditionally

Taking chance after chance,
We advance,
Without becoming victims of circumstance,
We hold the line,
As we hold our dissonance,
We hold those yellow boards,
Our boards of brilliance.

I'll Catch You Later

Even after every scripture,
Has been scripted,
Everyone is original,
Far from being encrypted,
So why do they want to patent people?

We only become aware,
Of what we're aware,
We can start at the ridiculous,
And then work our way backwards,
But once we're aware,
We can never go back there.

Trying to decipher,
Every dilemma,
Broken down,
Nothing seems real,
Digital has no feelings,
While labelled as digital.

Struggling to breathe,
Any faith in,
Or any fear out,
Still we're standing here,
At a pivotal moment within,
With the biggest grin,
Crying,
I'll catch you later.

Playing within the Kingdom of Heaven,
The whole gambit of experiences,
Within the chrysalis,
Of our metamorphosis,
We'll never miss,
Our lover's kiss.

We are defined,
As we're aligned,
Between difficulty and joy,
Attracting attention,
Spirits ahoy,
If we expect to see,
World War Three,
Oh boy,
It'll be here before we know it,
We can rearrange whatever is old,
With whatever is new,
If we allow it.

It's all about choice,
In what we choose,
Trust in yourself,
To yourself be true,
In all you pursue.

Revelation came after revelation,
Nobody needs anybody's representation,
After you have been through,
All you have been through,
God always knew,
You needed no validation,
Everything that was there,
Was always there,
For you.

Whatever happens,
Happens,
It will never break ya,
It's the smallest spark,
That will light up the darkness,
It's the little things in life,
That'll bring the most happiness.

After the long list of friends,
And foes,
There's few who ever got close enough,
To tread on your toes,
You were the one,
That marched on,
For the spirit in ya,
Cry hallelujah,
I'll catch you later.

Dilemma

If we never try,
Will we never know,
As we go trying to decipher,
Every dilemma,
Do we need things to get,
A little crazier?

As we're carrying on,
Like dust blowing in the wind,
Do existing beliefs,
Need to be re-examined,
Do we want a hysterectomy from freedom,
Do they directly control the weather,
Do we need an explanation,
For literally everything?

Whatever the situation,
Don't let your doubt die,
We get what we want,
While wanting to be certain,
Last year's conspiracies,
Are this year's truth,
The dilemma has always been,
The burden of proof.

It's as if we wanted to exist,
So badly,
Upon the two way street,
Of 'If Only',
But become lost in regretful confusion,
In the depths of despair,
It's painful to interact,
With someone's attachment to illusion.

We no longer say hell, o,
Until the whole belief system,
Is smashed to pieces,
And the disillusionment ceases.

How obvious,
Do things have to be,
Lets doubt until we discover,
The sacred key,
To enlightenment,
Pulled from the heaviest bunch,
From the dilemma of influence.

It can't just be a case,
Of I'm alright Jack,
Emphatically rejecting,
Every member of the public,
Where's the spiritual laws of alchemy,
Where are the minds of curiosity,
In our western society,
Where's the ascension of community?

It's hard to untangle,
The assumptions and hypothesis,
While being obligingly oblivious,
To the bloody obvious,
Our belief system,
Doesn't just up and leave,
There's little reprieve,
Until we know.

Every angel,
Has betrothed an angle,
To all that's on show,
As every page,
Will finally age,
Once it's let go.

We don't have to lose ourselves,
Chasing gold and silver,
Be gentle with yourself,
Kind words spoken are few,
The darkness has gone now,
The light of the light workers,
Grew and pushed through.

You're here,
For a reason,
To change the belief system
We used to know,
So do not fear,
Forgive,
Find peace within your soul,
It's up to you,
How you give it a go,
It's your dilemma.

The Way We Came In

A star is born,
Through the portal,
Of potential,
Sent from the Heavens to the Earth,
Born without judgement,
Expectations or obligations,
Just to breath is enough,
The mould has been broken,
From where we were taken.

Flawless imperfections,
Echoes from the hemispheres,
From another dimension,
From the in-between years,
There's a lot more to spiritualism,
Than just the way we came in.

Anything can happen,
To you,
Love life's collections,
Of flawless imperfections.

From the galaxy of stars,
From the substantial,
We go on to our own monumental scale,
We breathe into,
Our own treasure chest,
To exhale.

Breath is life,
The voice of God,
We've shone before,
What we have done,
Is done,
Could we have done more?

Bring back the blissful,
The light of love,
Vibrant colours become so vivid,
As we lift the lid,
We have a calling to call,
That opens the reservoirs,
In and out of our pores,
Flows the universal fluid,
Of consciousness.

We are all encompassing,
Everyone to everything,
And even the thin edge,
Of the wedge,
We can take on the chin,
Like the softest spontaneous sponge,
We take the plunge,
Taking everything in.

And we'll be crying forever,
Clinging like sea urchins,
To our flaws,
Too scared to rip off the gauze,
The gauze of regret,
A fool's only a fool,
If they forget,
The way they came in.

We're not here to keep repeating,
What went before,
Half a life,
Is half a life,
Reborn and reborn,
Presumed pseudonymous,
Of original reference,
Born again,
To make a difference.

Before we begin to crawl,
We want to know love,
In ancient Egypt,
Ancient Greece,
And ancient Rome,
We couldn't make much sense of it all,
Without love,
Life's past memories dwell.

A star is born,
Wrapped up in skin,
Do we really travel far,
From the way we came in?

In Your Arms

All of our tomorrows,
Are not promised by anyone,
Purpose over intent,
Are our tomorrows best spent,
Turning our selfish World,
Back into a selfless one?

It's all so encompassing,
In a world where we could have it all,
In mass and magnitude,
Construed inside an attitude,
Towards life.

We'll never recover,
From what the heck,
While living within the constraints,
Of someone's beguile,
It's like being kissed on the neck,
By a crocodile,
It doesn't end well.

Who has ever promised,
An everlasting smile,
But me,
While we're fighting for a life,
We may not get to see,
Believe me.

Third Time Truly Loving Unconditionally

As hard as I try,
There's somewhere an image,
Of what kind of fool am I,
As the weight of my entire lineage,
Will only deceive me,
In a world that is so demanding,
It ends with me,
And not a culturally conditioned society.

How can we ever take off,
If we keep thinking about the landing,
Let us all take off the mask,
That was once so poignantly comforting.

After almost,
Has almost gone,
Will we be catching our breath instead,
With that divine kiss on the forehead?

There's no redemption,
In the attention,
When we look in the mirror,
Is it us that we recognise,
Saint turning into a sinner,
In our experiences and mannerisms,
In our forever place,
That never stops moving,
We won't apologise.

Like a faded tattoo,
Even after we're gone,
We are still here,
In the memories we lived through,
In every grand rising,
Our sun shines on true,
Arise to survive,
Every impossible,
Our essence breathes us back,
Into something beautiful.

We are all with you,
In spirit,
Wrapped up in your memory,
We are embedded within it,
And that my dear friend,
Is a given,
We will be somewhere out there,
In your peripheral vision,
Like tumble weed rolling in silence,
Before it takes flight,
We are never that far out of sight.

It's alright me old mate,
It's alright,
There's the biggest smile upon my face,
As I just died in your arms tonight,
Thank you,
As I'm left as a residue,
In your warm embrace,
Surrounded by your grace.

Good Vibes

Sitting beneath,
The most beautiful dusk sky,
Our feelings fly,
After each sigh,
The whole jury is out,
In an unjust world,
Wanting to justify,
Until no one questions why,
We're on a high.

Picture tranquil fields,
Holding their patchwork,
Of daisies and daffodils,
Beneath the sky's light,
Of oranges, soft pinks and yellows,
We're high on the happy side,
Our hearts,
Flutter in flights that coincide,
Tonight's counterparts,
Are full of good vibes.

Just by being here,
We're on the up,
We'll always be guided,
By the chorus we sup.

Love's always provided,
To all and sundry miscellanea,
What's so life-affirming,
Is with continual learning,
No one falls down life's ascension escalator.

When we know we know,
We'll never miss,
The vital in vitalius,
What's essential, important and fundamental,
Like the Christ in Christina,
Love builds its crescendo,
To catch you later.

As we welcome one,
We welcome all,
Unconditional love's overflowing,
With every drop that we spill,
It all happens,
Simultaneously at will.

Love bursts the bubble of illusion,
Nothing real rarely exists,
Outside of love,
Your love,
My love,
It's the same manifestation,
Love is creation,
And love is here to thrive,
By being alive,
After every past trial and tribulation,
It still survives.

The beginning meant something different,
Then what it means now,
Looking back,
It had to happen this way,
To what extent,
Have we alluded to the argument,
That it will be okay?

Have we worked it out somehow,
Awakening the magnanimity of one's heart,
Every celestial event,
Comes from every celestial soul,
All that transpires,
Is as it is so,
We have to let go,
To depart.

Welcome to the new earth,
As it transcribes,
As we all play our part,
Manifesting good vibes.

Tomorrowland

All our best laid plans,
For Tomorrowland,
Awaking into a world of awareness,
Stirring from a lucid dream,
Into a conscious state,
Somewhere in limbo between Heaven and Hell,
It's hard to tell,
Who's thankful for gratefulness,
Without any intention to indicate,
Good things come to those who wait,
Or choose the good things collectively,
With natural propensity.

Are we giving the World away,
Do we often consider,
Achieving all that we need,
Without greed,
Do we care that much,
Tomorrowland is somehow out of touch,
As we keep hoping that something better,
Is just around the corner.

It's coming,
It's coming,
It's coming,
Something better,
Than you ever planned for,
When we love one another,
As well as the future,
Hallelujah,
Hallelujah,
Hallelujah.

We're no longer,
Half a world away,
Raising our spiritual temperatures,
We behave in a certain way.

When we particularly deliver the truth,
From chakra to chakra,
We appreciate everything,
Within the labyrinth of our mind,
We are each choice we make,
Each change,
In which we partake.

We are the beginning of something,
We know nothing about,
We find as we find,
As what has always happened,
Has always been,
From the holograms of hallucinations,
You're on of the clearest visions,
That we've ever seen.

Nothing is accidental,
We are where we are,
We've travelled through potentials portal,
Across many lifetimes,
Repeating what we are unwilling,
To let go,
Let's not become a version,
Of someone we don't even know.

Right now,
Life is for the living,
And that's a good reason,
To dismantle the politico,
We don't need to be governed,
By indoctrinations,
Poisons,
And contracts of control.

Words are just words,
Until they are the words,
That we live by,
Today we can testify,
That we can stand in our power,
Hand in hand,
Hour by hour,
We will create,
Our own Tomorrowland.

Abnormal

The Universe,
In chapter and verse,
Is pulsing energy,
Right through our veins,
There is no normality,
In broken DNA chains.

If you're feeling strongly,
That chaos is coming,
The heaviness gets hard,
Filled with anxiety,
With a sense of foreboding,
After each wayward viewing,
Of the news,
No news is good news.

Our faith calls for a leap,
A quantum leap,
Within our on off arbitrary conceptions,
It's unstoppable in deleting deceptions,
The cluster of squadrons,
Of what goes around,
Comes around.

We need each other,
More than ever,
There's no expiration date,
On our own logic,
That something is coming,
And that something is catastrophic.

Transhumanism,
The fourth industrial revolution,
This doom is coming,
The doom sayers say,
The light bearers,
Shed light on each situation,
Do you want confirmation,
That God is watching,
We know it's only the surface,
That we've been scratching,
We are the barometers,
Of what is happening.

We are shifting,
From ego to soul,
From personality to authentic self,
It's a humbling experience,
Being surrounded by tyranny,
We don't need any leader ship,
That only leads to dictatorship.

Self sabotage,
Comes after the camouflage,
Of our own entourage,
It's us,
We are the ones
We have been looking for.

But fools rush in,
Where wise men,
Fear to tread,
In the race for survival,
It's our abnormality,
For sustainability,
That's become widespread,
Into a world,
Where nothing and nobody,
Is normal.

We are the seekers of the truth,
Searching for a light,
At the end of the tunnel,
Tormented,
And torn apart,
We pray for those,
Lost in the night,
Who disappeared in the dark.

We cry out,
We are here,
For those,
Who can't be here,
For those who didn't stand a chance,
For the victims of circumstance.

How can it be,
With CCTV surveillance everywhere,
That so many children,
Go missing each year,
After all the loving and searching,
Why are thousands of children,
Still somehow missing.

We cry,
To bring them back home,
Our lions' roars,
Rocks the foundation,
That leads to Rome,
We have been fighting,
What's wrong,
This unexplained dread,
As so many,
Have been carrying on,
Walking upon,
The skulls and bones of the dead.

What will come,
Is paranormally coming,
Even at times,
When it becomes exhausting.

We are driven
We are in it for the long haul,
To expose what's been hidden,
Everything,
Everywhere,
Will be exposed,
For once and for all,
We will abolish,
What has been abnormal.

Parasite Cleansing

The worse it gets,
The closer we get,
To the whole thing collapsing,
We are parasite cleansing,
For the health of our souls,
And the souls of our ancestors,
Cleansing ourselves from all the ill will,
And malice,
Till the restoration of peace,
The restoration of justice.

We're on a mission,
Of changing,
What went before,
Parasite cleansing,
Every bugbear,
Others opinions,
Inaccurate conclusions,
To understanding ourselves,
There's no conclusion.

When the drip,
Becomes a trickle,
Ludicrous ideas continue and continue,
Until the flood becomes global.

Each system is built up on,
Fraud, lies and deception,
In all its malicious selection,
No one gets close,
To winning an election,
We are washing away,
Every fake expression.

When our inner voice,
Is continually calling,
We can't keep on pretending,
Like we don't care,
About what's behind,
Every creation,
Every tortured human expression,
We can't allow the dehumanisation,
The eternal domination,
Behind every cajole,
From the crouching dark shadows,
That are lurking behind,
Each human soul.

What we are feeling,
Is our consciousness calling,
For a level playing field,
For every lie,
To be revealed,
As old layers of insurrection,
Are painfully peeled,
For the inspection,
Of old wounds,
That can finally become healed,
The past,
Cannot be buried underground,
Any more,
What's lying underground,
Can no longer be contained,
Or profoundly concealed.

We're living through
These crazy times,
Where nothing is normal,
Nothing is fine,
With crazy staged events,
Arranged by anonymous sources,
These global criminals,
Corruption networks,
Work on demonic courses
And their puppet presidents,
Of bloodline descendants.

Their warmongering,
Their backward thinking,
The college,
Of every fateful encounter,
They are the enemy,
They are the saboteur,
Behind the gates,
Prolonging war.

We are our own free will,
We won't let,
One drop of blood spill,
Over the grotesque insanity,
Of inhuman slaughter,
We are the guardians,
Of the land, air and water,
We won't bow down to any body,
With Gods given law,
We can all say no,
To war.

None the less,
We are blessed,
With a backbone,
We can stand up,
With righteousness,
Life's not just about existing,
Within a physical body,
Daily dodging the bullets,
Of parasitical tyranny.

Our souls,
Are supervening,
Each one of life's pretensions,
Doing the best,
We can do,
Facing what's hurting,
Love's reasserting
As we find peace,
By parasite cleansing,

Cosmic Crackles

There's a hum,
Across the hemispheres,
A buzzing frequency in translation,
A ringing in our ears.

It happens simultaneously,
Every possibility,
Is exponentially increasing,
Our path of following through with intention,
It's a constant communication.

Along our process of ascension,
Is our cosmic crackle,
Increasing our ability,
To awaken spiritual guidance,
From different worlds,
From different dimensions.

We're doing the best,
With what we've got,
Whether we do,
Or we do not,
Tune into,
Another point of view,
From ours to theirs,
We try to connect with,
A different perspective.

We're crying out with idiosyncrasies,
Every dis,
From every disease,
We are akin to each injustice,
Actions have their consequences.

Why are we conditioned to think,
Without thinking,
We know that life is risky,
As they're pushing mental health,
Conditions of safety,
From what they foresee,
As the madness of the future,
Stressing us so we can't think clearly.

Losing ourselves,
To find ourselves,
Separated from a past that we've forgotten,
Alienated and medicated,
Regulated, uneducated and indoctrinated,
Why would we ever consider,
Playing Russian roulette with our children,
This can't go on,
Injection after injection,
With another unknown quantity of poison.

We can't inject health,
Into the healthy,
By piercing the porous protection,
Of the skin,
The science behind this,
Is beyond me.

Our minds are more powerful,
Than any surgeon's scalpel,
And the cellular atoms within us,
Are traceable to the stars,
Pulsating and resonating,
While continually fluctuating,
Back to our cores,
Like invisible treacle,
Our cosmic crackle,
Resolutely restores.

Expectancy is everywhere,
The more that we're aware,
The hairs stand to attention,
On the back of our necks,
We repair whatever is broken,
As we've awoken,
From whatever is next.

Within our own doctrinaire,
Of prayer,
Speaking our own truths,
Without compare,
As we amend,
We all transcend.

We're blessed,
As we tap into the oneness,
Of our cosmic ampere of universal love,
Somewhere from above,
It's been whispering,
Shifting the shackles,
Our cosmic heart beats,
To the cosmic crackles.

When The Sides Become Side less

Isolated,
Within a million square miles,
Within an isolated world,
Within a fabricated world,
For many of the majority,
It really is a very small world.

They lie,
They cover up and censor,
Words have been translated,
And mutilated,
Way before the Magna Carta,
We've paid the price,
Ten times over,
We've paid the Pied Piper.

What game is it,
That we are playing,
From the hyper-consumerist,
To the hyper-individualist,
Mindless compulsions and addictions,
Heads deep within,
'I can't believe it',
Denials,
We keep on dismissing,
Our relationship trials.

So many with a craving,
Self-centred saving,
Jumping ship,
To be on the winning side,
Without any conviction,
Just to disconnect,
With wilful neglect,
And dereliction,
Nothing is simple,
Within our ecosystem.

There isn't an ism,
That wasn't a division,
That we didn't fight,
Tyrannical,
Nonsensical lockdowns,
That changed over night,
District to district,
Who are we really,
If we don't get to choose,
Who we want to be?

Has it finally clicked,
When science and technology,
Are running out of control,
God's domain has the therapy,
To heal every soul
Divine intervention is happening,
God is stepping in.

Collectively we were meant,
To find each other,
With respect and dignity,
And to live in freedom,
Everybody makes a society,
When the sides become side less,
It will happen naturally.

Which side of history,
Will we be on,
If we keep repeating history,
There's no peace for anyone.

There's no place to hide,
When no one is satisfied,
Every divide,
Is no longer real,
Insanity,
Selectively grows within our profanity.

Darkness versus light,
Good versus evil,
Time's up,
The clock has always been ticking,
We smell it,
We hear it,
We see it,
We feel it.

If we throw are ego away,
If we throw the narrative away,
To act as one,
Togetherness is really sticking,
By the side of each fellow human,
Together we are powerful,
Divided we fall.

There's no real side that we were ever on,
The balance of life,
Is where we belong,
Like pebbles on the beach,
We've been washed up to teach,
Everyone to get along.

Why do we label others intentions,
Trying to make some sense of it all,
For us to forever egress,
Each side dissolves,
As Pluto,
Jumps into the age of Aquarius
Astronomically all of humanity evolves,
Until we all become side less,
Back to what we know.

When It Whispers In Your Ear

From a very high vibration,
We've heard the word,
Whispered into our ears,
We are now collectively reaching everyone,
All the souls that weren't aware,
The word has escalated undeterred,
Far away from the invisible puppeteers.

Everything starts from something,
There's no separation from somewhere,
Our quantum leap has occurred,
Now that we've remembered,
What it's like to be alive,
There's no fear.

Expressed experience is our experience,
Of the mystical and literal in combination,
All the languages of division,
All the metaphors that are hidden,
Within religion,
Become clear,
We are moving on up,
Away from here,
Away from their living hell,
There's no place for fear,
To dwell.

We're moving away,
From their lower frequencies,
From the monstrosities of corrupted energies,
From their dark entities,
We have turned off their power,
Turning confusion into clarity.

We're shedding light on each situation,
We're aligning with kindness,
Near, far and everywhere,
Our phenomenal power,
Is immeasurable,
In curing the incurable.

Energetically perpetuating light,
From tonight,
To the end of time,
Spinning within our vortex,
A million times over,
We go on,
Codex from another codex.

The code of consciousness,
Whispers in our ears,
Until we take note,
That the word is love,
And love is the antidote to fear.

Blessed beyond belief,
On our healing journey,
Love's duration is never brief,
It's inspiration and imagination,
Everything's a relationship,
Everything's a form of communication.

As we float along,
Upon the sea of experience,
We hang on,
As our vessels bob,
Up and down a bit,
But we won't let our anchors slip,
If we listen,
To the intertwining words,
That make our love grow,
Underneath the mistletoe,
Of emotions that we knit.

Love is you,
And you are everywhere,
Love always whispers,
Into your ear.

Eternally The Same

Energy from another energy,
Fire, water, air and earth,
Physical elements elementary,
Eternally,
Simply,
The same.

Once man renounces reason,
How much is enough,
How can we,
Dismiss anything,
Anything outside,
The experience we're having?

Believing in something,
Is different,
From having a theory,
Which is different,
From knowing completely.

When we know knowledge,
Can never be complete,
But through truth,
What's indiscreet,
What's beyond anyone's comprehension,
Will one day be reached,
Through ascension.

The metamorphosis of supposition,
Has now packed its bags,
It's long gone,
What's real,
What kind of web has been spun?

You can see my face,
But can you see me,
When I claim to be,
By divine design,
Each fact becomes a fallacy,
After the great reveal,
Of our manufactured reality,
It comes back to what we know,
It's all about soul.

Together in all its glory,
Everybody has their own love story,
Determined undeterred,
It's the greatest we've ever heard.

Our miracle is found in our profundities,
In our greatest essentialities,
Of greatness,
Of sameness.

We are the same,
We are the light,
We are the power,
We are the spirit within,
We are the Kingdom of Heaven,
We never quit,
We never give in,
We are the sisters,
We are the brethren,
Let our story begin.

Bursting through the limits,
Of our visible world,
It's worth starting over,
Bringing in the light in its love,
The same,
But one word would not exist,
Without the other,
Bringing it back together,
All the mountains and valleys,
All the laughter and tears,
A common purpose within us rallies,
All the hope,
All the prayers.

Does anything or anyone ever differ,
As we're choosing what we would prefer,
What becomes different,
In its differentiation,
In its manifestation?

The written word,
Will hold no shame,
It's there for ever,
As it poetically remains,
Eternally the same.

Safe Haven

Why does doubt,
Have the strange habit,
Of collecting shadows,
All the wounds we don't admit?

Diligently we refuse,
What we refuse,
Will we ever diligently choose,
To walk within,
Another's shoes?

The pain of searing loss,
Every comparison comes with a cost,
It's hard to sleep with one eye open,
While dreaming that,
The door to our own destruction,
Has both of its hinges,
Permanently broken,
It seems like every foot soldier,
Is seeking safe haven.

It's been a real eye opener,
That whatever comes from,
Some World Economic Forum contributor,
Is designed for control,
It will never make our life any easier.

Safe haven is rarely found,
In the familiarity,
Of safety and security,
It isn't about locking ourselves away,
Or going in lock step with another country.

Life's a risk taking,
Vast adventure,
We know every bad storm,
Won't last forever.

What is it that we're putting by,
For a rainy day,
From cradle to grave,
What is it that we are stuffing,
Under the eiderdown,
What is it that we can save,
From financial meltdown?

Nothing is wasted,
After the moment,
Our matter changed,
Before that moment mattered.
Are our hotels full,
Have they reached their limit,
In life's merry go round,
In life's crazy circus,
We forgive those who trespass,
Against us.

Why don't we shout from the rooftops,
About what's kept extremely quiet,
We are fighting the fourth industrial revolution,
With the fifth dimension resolution.

When we can't wait to move on,
Time asks no questions,
In its own progression,
Inhaling and exhaling creates the vacuum,
To the cause and effect phenomenon.

We came into this realm,
To deliver us from evil,
To our safe haven,
We have our universal laws,
Of what dreams may come.

The battle between good and evil,
Masculinity fights for elbow room,
On the opportunities table,
Like Kane versus Able,
There has to be a recognition,
Of opposition.

Within the World and its matrix,
Our DNA is our DNA,
Forever and ever,
Not to become,
Rewritten,
In some transhumanist agenda,
We will treasure,
Our purity within,
The light of our authentic,
Safe haven.

World Without End

Good on us,
Good on them,
Who speaks of winning,
In the beginning,
Before we've even started to win?

Who believes in us,
Who believes in anyone,
We go out into the World,
To do what we've got to do,
Not knowing that we've already won,
Well before the validation,
Of well done?

Not one of us,
Will be fighting for an ending,
When we realise,
Nothing is over,
Nothing is done,
How many of us,
Have thrown a spanner,
Right into the works of Armageddon,
Honesty is the best policy,
In this place of lies,
When somebody dies,
Their library of love,
Does not die with them.

Their words,
Their world goes on,
Their wisdom without end,
Echoes through past prayers,
In their hopes and dreams,
Where everybody cares,
We have been blessed,
To be tied at the seams,
Standing shoulder to shoulder,
Our fingers entwined with theirs.

Beside them,
We became,
Who we became,
Enhancing the World,
The World without end,
With the compassion and courage,
Of those who have influenced us.

My friend,
Every place,
Every story,
Every hope,
Every glory,
It makes a difference,
To our own inventory.

The spirit in each story,
Holds on to its remembrance,
Chances come forth,
After we take the chance,
Which in turn,
Turns into tomorrow's guidance.

Irreplaceable,
While still traceable,
Are all those wrinkles of wisdom,
From our walking,
Talking,
Encyclopedias,
Our older generation,
The curious inquirers,
That kept darkness at bay,
For whom ever appears throughout history,
Historically has had their say.

Evolution starts somewhere,
Within its backwards love,
For whom holds the evidence of history,
Holds the conclusion of hereof.

In their footprints,
That they leave behind,
Enriched with a lifetime of experience,
Their memories will cross,
Each unbridgeable void,
Of people, places and things,
That were once destroyed.

Along life's long conveyor belt,
Of gold, oil and drugs,
Has the pattern been replaced,
On those worn out rugs?

Is the hand that we're given,
Already bitten,
By the hand of fate,
From the very last supper,
To the very last meal,
Will we get to see,
What's actually real,
Before the symbolism,
Within the curriculum,
Is dealt?

Something is screaming,
Something is offhand,
Is this all too much,
For us to comprehend,
Within this World,
Our World without end?

Echoes

Derivative of where,
Or whence it came,
Word weaving,
Is just as deceiving,
Without proof,
Without claim.

With the might of the pen,
The renegades,
Throw the hand grenades,
Into the pit of deception,
It's blown wide open,
All that's dystopian,
The collapse of civilisation,
The civil unrest,
The social instability,
In its own absolution,
Who's validating our own reality,
With divine justice as the solution?

Manipulated by outside forces,
Prophesying is false,
Without the consequences,
Echoes of ones self,
Are shown through our ancestry,
I can't tell you about your tomorrows,
Without a quest for clarity,
What's coming in its ambiguity,
Inside numerology and sacred geometry,
Astrology and every other combined theory,
We find the guilty,
Where belief becomes the enemy.

Unsurpassed,
With little to cherish,
As we perish the thought,
Of what our forefathers fought,
Those echoes,
Those foes,
From the past.

We're no longer,
Shaking a spear,
At what's insincere
Or casting a shadow,
Over tomorrow.

There's no definition,
From whence they came,
The hierarchy,
The monarchy,
They have no true identity,
They have no real authority,
They have no intention,
Of ever liberating humanity.

It's all down to us,
To break free,
From the bifurcation branches,
Of our insidious past
Those slings and arrows,
Have now come to pass.

Redemption draws nigh,
There's no need for a king,
As we are saved,
From deep rooted sin,
We begin to rectify,
Each soul on Schindler's list,
We all coexist,
With our perplexing minds,
Every alchemist,
Mixes the pot,
With most things combined.

The whole lot,
Is a lot to take in,
But with repeated echoes,
Of mindful reflection,
Decades of connections,
Inside the genes,
From your cosmic clan,
You've got this,
You can handle this,
You know you can.

Where are we going,
Won't be,
Where we have gone,
Santification,
Goes euphorically on.

In our,
Wibbly wobbly world,
It's all much to do about nothing,
If what we are doing,
Is done without feeling,
Is done without meaning,
Then what is it
We are doing it for?

Faith and insanity,
Are like sister and brother,
From some long lost family,
Teasing each other,
Eventually we will get to know them,
By their moral character.

Isn't it all meant to be,
Just as you like it,
Don't we,
Now know
To jump away from the snake,
Before we are bit,
The Kingdom of Heaven,
Is in our own hands,
As we test the spirit,
All the echoes within it,
Protect our DNA strands.

Stand In The Park

We stand in our truth,
And never expect anything less,
If we don't stand up for the children,
Then who are we,
If we don't fight for their freedom,
Then who are we?

With each heart to heart,
We dismantle the dark,
To prebunk,
To debunk,
The darkness.

We can put the whole world to rights,
Lightworkers standing up for their rites,
It's the dawn of a new paradigm,
Away from the own nothing,
And be happy pantomime.

The pendulum of thought,
Swings from what's wrong,
To whatever is now wrong,
It's the richest elites,
That stay in the background,
Where they,
Are nowhere to be found,
As history repeats,
Their mission to depopulate,
Who are they,
Is what we now contemplate?

Yes we have the puppet philanthropists,
That always insist,
They have a solution to that,
They have a solution to this,
They assert that we must lower the carbon,
To make this World a better place,
Knowing that we are the carbon,
They say it with a grin on each face.

The majority of the mainstream,
Are flowing down stream,
Without a paddle,
Heading for the greatest fall,
The majority of the mainstream,
Are on a motorbike ride,
Unable to swallow their pride,
They're riding side saddle,
Unable to come to grips with it all.

They are trying to kill us,
How can we reason with this,
When the rich always win,
And the poor have no justice?

In the park we have a gathering,
To hug like we mean it,
In the dewy tears of the morning,
Fingermarks are left,
Imprinted on backs,
Away from the theft of those censorships,
We reform companionships,
With every grand rising.

We are blessed at the moment,
We know we're blessed,
None of us are lost,
We have survived the holocaust.

We will build our own tribe,
Without the patriarch,
We stand in the park,
We stand in the countryside,
Side by side.

Serenity Inside The Storm

Whatever could be,
Whatever should be,
How long do we have to wait,
For us to proceed,
We have to get over,
Over our greed,
To focus on what's really here,
Nature will never take more,
Than it needs.

We have unlimited power,
The ambiguity of a never ending story,
We are ducking and diving,
In our ability to stay alive,
While surviving.

It comes in spits and spurts,
Those emergency broadcast systems,
Cast their alarms,
Cast their alerts.

How do we live in the now,
In a place where materialism,
Has nothing to treasure,
Denying our future,
Would be like living,
As a fish out of water.

Who holds a hug for humanity,
In our humble love,
Decisions are limitless,
As our future is guessed,
We all go on to manifest,
What we want to be,
As we navigate these times,
With compassion and empathy,
The path that we take,
Is one of serenity.

The storm only lasts,
As long as we let it,
Anything can happen,
And anything hasn't happened yet,
A spiritual shift,
Happens right where we are standing,
Singularities and disparities,
Are quickly disbanding.

Collectively we smash open,
The pinata of dreams,
Each conscious shift,
Is a colossal gift,
Giving us a chance to write our own story,
The story is over and done,
If everybody's is a harmless one.

As we harmonise with peace in our hearts,
We hold a fantastic future,
As the future starts,
No one's superior,
No one's inferior,
Everybody is free,
To love thy neighbour.

Serenity is found in its own serenity,
It's somewhere where the truth truly dwells,
Where there are no goodbyes,
Only farewells.

Resonates

Ready for anything,
Ready for everything,
What resonates,
Stimulates a move,
Inside the movement,
All those unforeseeable experiences,
We are yet to experience,
Does it make a difference,
That anything to everything,
Is not as it appears to be,
That everything's alive,
Connected with energy?

As we are dealing with the consequences,
That so often occur,
Our polarity within life's journey,
Makes the tumultuous time,
Fly by in a blur.

Do we get what we're giving,
As those energy siphons,
Like to suck the life out of the living,
All those energy vampires,
It only goes to show ya,
As it transpires,
That loving yourself is a must,
We are the one's that teach others,
How to treat us.

Believe in yourself,
Believe in your love,
As you are the greatest relationship,
That you'll ever have,
Do unto others,
As you would want them,
To do unto you,
We can all go above and beyond,
Whatever resonated,
In the World we once knew.

We go on forever,
For worse or for better,
We came into this World made out of love,
It's the truth searcher that seeks,
Whatever resonates,
What culminates,
With love.

Either way it is us,
We came here to forgive,
However we live,
We can give ourselves some grace,
After each time we are coerced,
How many regrets are ever reversed,
As everyone's bubble,
Eventually gets burst.

How far we've come,
Leaving footprints behind,
In shifting sands,
We aren't here to play their game,
As we roll the dice,
It's out of their hands.

Whatever resonates,
Will resonate,
From here to thereof,
To right out from our soul,
We came here to love,
Throughout the World,
Without an end goal.

Our hearts will go on,
We will always love,
What resonates for everyone,
Is endless love,
Unconditional love.

Circles Of Souls

There has to be so much more,
Than what's gone before,
With many more wonders to behold,
Like empathy, mercy and conscience,
All of which are priceless,
And cannot be sold.

Earthlings that hold no space for evil,
Are lifting the veil,
With an uprising,
To see what's behind artificial intelligence,
Nothing can be hidden,
As serious secrets grow closer to the Sun,
The darkness is exposed,
Just before it is gone.

We can't turn a blind eye,
To what we feel,
Energetically,
We have the responsibility,
To protect our souls with the armour of God,
To deliver ourselves from evil,
From each deception and fraud,
From the judge that holds the gavel.

We shall not be judged,
Nor will we judge,
We can look at it,
From a different angle,
We know now what is good for us,
In this age of Aquarius.

It's moving in circles,
Moving so fast,
Those that push the green agenda,
Will sooner or later,
Sit down to a banquet,
Of consequences,
Chewing on evil propaganda.

Living in fifteen minute cities,
That have nowhere to go,
Dividing everywhere into districts,
Keeping the circle of souls,
Under control.

Fine upon fine,
Nothing is fine,
There's no justification for climate change,
When it's all by design.

Being confined to urban areas,
Where you can't travel far,
Won't stop the turning of karma's wheel,
When our greatest revelations,
Add fuel to the fire,
To shed light onto the greatest reveal.

Whatever we fear,
Is the fear we have to face,
Life is for living,
Whatever is the case.

We are where we're supposed to be,
Believe in yourself without validation,
Study yourself,
Look within to your intentions,
Trials and tribulations,
Help us foresee,
That giving up was never our option.

We won't sell our souls,
To meet evil halfway,
We won't pay the reaper,
Or be lead astray,
After lifetimes and lifetimes,
Of knowing the score,
The circles of souls,
Has come back once more.

Approximation

What's really going on,
Is this going to be,
Our final swan song,
Is it all just an approximation,
Is it a simulation?

As retrogressions,
Keep going backwards,
From our worst case scenario,
Have they brainwashed us simultaneously,
As strange anomalies,
Become hard to discuss,
In our pursuit to become whole,
Our attachments should never drown us.

There's so many different snippets of information,
From so many different multiple sources,
The destruction just carries on,
What are the chances,
We will get out alive,
With electric magnetic pulses,
What's the approximation,
Of how many will survive?

How long do any of us,
Really have left,
If they are poisoning the water and the air,
It's in our hydration,
It's in our last breath.

These multiple levels of attack,
On good people,
With cyber surveillance weapons,
Of mass destruction,
Are hell bent on population reduction.

Isn't it about time,
We all questioned why,
We are trying to ignore,
The same pesky fly,
Yes,
We all live our lives,
Until we pass on and die,
But why,
Are so many,
Dying so suddenly,
So unexpectedly?

It's like they're weaponising,
The health care system,
As we now,
Have to protect the body,
From every invasion,
Every bio weapon.

It's no surprise,
When we look to the skies,
Micro dust now frequently roams,
It's just part of the long list,
That gets dismissed,
While we live amongst,
The insanity,
Of sudden death syndromes.

These are just a few,
Of the crimes,
Against humanity,
What are you,
Going to do,
In these unprecedented times?

We don't have a legitimate government,
They've gone rogue,
Treating us like canaries,
Down in the coal mines,
Still this destruction goes on,
In its prevailing vogue,
Of each and every divide,
With the truths they hide.

What side,
Of history,
Will we be on,
If history its self,
Has historically lied?

Pinch Yourself

What is it,
That we are supposed to do,
Keep paying into the system,
Until the system finally kills you?

Do we just sit back and take it,
Pinching ourselves,
Until we're black and blue,
Praying,
That they're not just out for themselves,
While collecting,
Their inland revenue?

Is this revolution,
In civilisation,
Just counterfeit,
Are we trying to leave our World,
In a better shape,
Than we found it?

It's a Brobdingnagian feat,
When the majority don't know,
What shape the World is,
Under their feet.

There's robots and drones,
Surveying our homes,
There's insects as food,
With Frankenlab meat,
It's right in our faces,
It's not discreet.

With eyes looking through the letterbox,
They won't keep away the rapture,
When the rapture knocks,
It deprives, chastises and demoralises,
Until it really hurts,
Redemption is a dish that only relishes,
Our just desserts.

Everybody knows somebody,
That is so easily coercible,
For so many Masonic years,
Their financiers have broad cast,
What they want to last,
Their intentions to depopulate,
Is it now irreversible?

Has the damage been done,
Is it now too late,
When will enough be enough,
When they have ripped up the Bible,
Be informed before leaving Earth,
What's happening now,
Is something that's biblical.

Facial recognition,
Ai,
Automation,
Where our mobile phones,
Are our identification,
The truth becomes something,
That so many hide,
When they have stopped caring about the truth,
Only caring about what side,
They will be on.

Come on,
Wake up,
Pinch yourself,
This ain't about money,
This ain't about wealth,
In our land of milk and honey,
It's about our mental health.

If it doesn't happen now,
Do you think it'll happen,
In another afterlife,
Please pinch yourself,
Pinch your own consciousness,
Back into life.

Caught Up Within The Courts

Truth draws strength from itself,
The discernment,
Won't recognise the adjournment,
Until we know ourselves,
Are true to ourselves,
Become responsible in responding,
Be more understanding.

There's no ifs,
Or buts,
For all and sundry,
Underneath the snowball of lies,
We're corresponding,
To someone's disguise,
What justifies,
Justifies,
What jurisdiction we're under.

After years of indoctrination,
With no real turnaround,
The nations dumbfounded,
Spell bounded,
Who in their right mind,
Wants to be ruled, schooled,
And fooled,
They pin a medal of mediocrity,
On every lapel that laps it up,
Two worlds existing simultaneously.

We now know,
How little we know,
What was once hidden,
Shows its transparency,
We're now in the midst of conquering,
Somewhere we've never been,
Somewhere in-between,
The robin and the rainbow.

What's it going to take,
To break the contract behind each contraction,
To break the legalese,
Designed to appease,
The ease of each verdict,
The peace of God's law,
Sorry is the only word to contradict,
Each action,
That went before,
No one's ever sorry before each interaction.

Public servants become subservient,
Within the fake facilities,
That facilitate,
Unrelenting syndicates,
Run for the hills,
Misrepresenting magistrates,
Play their game,
In the name,
Of the Crown,
Their poison spills,
Our reasons have already been shut down,
Without compromise,
By the hands of corporations,
Psychopaths have the last word,
Lies beget more lies.

Every stimulus,
To their commotion less fuss,
Within their propaganda encyclopedia,
Holds no perspective,
Holds no contempt,
No authority,
Is free from liability,
Or made exempt.

Our struggle,
Is man made deliberately,
Someone somewhere always seems to be,
Silently suffering,
Every bruised chakra,
Is crying,
Out to ya,
To live under God's law,
To be diligent in discovery.

Let's be there for one another,
Let's stand up for our rights,
Nothing is more important,
Than to help one another.

That voice that's lingering inside,
Every chant,
That's crying out,
Is justified,
This could be our last resort,
To break free of what lasts,
Let's sort out the corruption,
Inside the courts.

Inevitable

The costumes we wear,
Of our overindulgence,
Weigh heavy upon,
Every victim of circumstance,
Why are so many completely oblivious,
To what's going on?

We are facing infinity,
Without even flinching,
In this spiritual war,
We can't keep letting,
The war keep on winning,
Bereft of life,
Before we are living.

What are we made of,
What is are use,
Where do we begin,
When we are let loose?

We are not an approximation,
Of a human being,
Spending our lives protected,
In some kind of inhuman crèche,
Our love for one another,
Isn't something that we ration,
We are here giving everything,
Here in the flesh.

We are everything,
In this electromagnetic,
Psychological storm,
We are all in recovery,
As we perform.

We try to see the bigger picture,
But it goes by,
In the blink of an eye,
It doesn't matter how hard we try,
How hard we fight it,
The battle of good versus evil,
Is never over,
If it isn't started.

It's not about being clever,
It's not about being smart,
It's about that gut feeling,
Every heart to heart.

Let's give those silent battles,
Something to talk about,
It's the ones,
That didn't go along with it all,
That were labelled delusional,
But the truth comes out in the end,
It's inevitable,
My friend.

Every district has zones,
That hold their consequences,
5G should be taken down,
As it attacks the senses,
Let's look up from our phones,
From these smart technologies.

Smart meters,
Smart cities,
Leaving little that's left,
To the imagination,
In a World that's so wonderful and vast,
Why would anyone ask,
For a virtual representation?

There may come a day,
When every thing we do,
Needs identification,
And everywhere we go,
Is tracked by location,
There's no going back,
To where we've come from,
Don't be controlled,
Or live in isolation.

Make your own choice,
You know what feels right,
We are all going to move on,
So live your best life.

The Universe has lifted,
Us away from tragedy,
We have been gifted,
A life with morality.

It's the greatest time to be alive,
It's inevitable,
That we will get there,
When we arrive.

Saving Grace

Awe inspiring moments,
Come from small beginnings,
From little letters,
From a big place,
When the people show us,
Who they are,
We've come so far,
From where we were,
Beyond the heartbreak of saving grace.

From poverty to riches,
Slaves to whatever is monetary,
It doesn't serve us well,
Sir,
I remain a slave no more,
What's happening now,
Wasn't happening before.

Killing off the straw man identity,
As each corporation falls,
We go forth,
Into the land of milk and honey,
That's true for sure,
In this spiritual war.

Everyone is a contender,
We will never begin to start on over,
Without throwing something else away,
Come as they will,
Come as they may.

There before the grace of God,
Go I,
"I",
Is not the individual,
It's the healing potential,
Of everyone.

The eye of Horus,
It's when the collective consciousness,
Rises up in humanity,
For a different reality,
A different dimension,
A different frequency,
Third time truly,
Loving unconditionally,
Under our Sun.

We will find grace,
In living life gracefully,
It's literally liberating,
Counting our blessings,
The beating of our hearts,
Are echoing,
Within,
The peoples' diary,
The truth will set us free,
In all it's glory,
In each poem's story,
Of love.

Traditions fall,
By the wayside,
The hidden agendas,
Have no where to hide,
Our love is all around,
Keep sharing the love,
Our love.

Cometh the hour,
Cometh the man,
Come every single moment,
Saving grace every way we can,
Throwing pebbles,
Into the pond of confusion,
Waves of abundance,
Grow in anticipation,
Eager to walk the path,
Of higher intention.

We keep on,
Keeping on,
We change the World,
That we once knew,
Our messages and energies,
Ripple out to all the people,
Dispelling evil,
Saving grace,
Not for one,
But for all.

We show the way,
We find in our hearts,
The words to say,
I love you.

Shackles Of Society

In this polarised world of extremes,
There's little sympathy,
From those who post,
More's the pity memes,
From those who couldn't care less,
So stuck in their ways,
Stuck in their acquiesce,
Finding derogative ways to impress,
Stuck in the nothingness.

In this dystopian man made hell,
Our inauthentic society,
The media will feed ya,
Psychological intrusions,
All the latest scoops,
To break humanity,
Through calamity's hoops.

In their MK ultra mind control,
Of illusions,
That has society,
Jumping with conformity,
With each submission,
Can we ditch the enemy,
The opposition,
It's designed to suppress the spirit,
Suppress the soul.

Can we ditch social media,
It couldn't get any meaner,
Pretending the grass is greener,
Changing freedom forever,
Taking energies away from good souls,
It's a monstrous attack,
By faceless trolls.

Every misdemeanour will affect everyone,
The Governments insidious acts,
Of terrorism,
On those standing up for their freedom,
There's no in-between,
When everything's broken.

Right now,
Is the most important time,
In humanities history,
As we call for a collective change,
For freedom from the shackles of society,
We call for the light workers,
The warriors,
The truth seekers,
And healers,
That are here for the duration,
The pure of heart,
That won't depart.

From the power within,
Our last hurrah,
Let us free our fictional roles,
Within their theatre of commerce,
Lost in their lawless sea,
Let our army of unalienable rights,
Fight their maritime admiralty.

Let the presumption of joinder,
Get tossed out of the window,
As we get to know natural law,
The right to life,
Freedom and happiness,
The right to contract or not in our business,
The right to travel each country,
The right to our privacy and confidentiality.

We were born into this World,
Without a birth,
And so much was taken,
Before a rattle was shaken,
Before we knew our worth.

It's time to say no,
To the indoctrination,
The scam,
Of working for the man,
That way has no salvation,
The incorporation of culture,
Has no future,
Let's free ourselves from the shackles of society,
Finally for sure.

Controversial

The great pitcher of memories,
Pours as she pours,
It's just the beginning,
Of a flood of memories,
That wash up on our shores.

A new planetary frequency,
Some kind of paranormal activity,
Is here to save humanity,
New intentions,
Arrive from other dimensions,
As we discover,
Some of our oldest origins.

Something is out there,
Something is coming,
It resolutely reveals,
What's beyond the Antarctic,
And how our civilisation feels,
Consequentially cosmic,
As our Andromedans,
Pleiadians, Sirians and Arcturians,
Now work their magik.

We are now open to the possibility,
Of realising how little we know,
And that we could be wrong,
In all that we believe,
For what it is worth,
What have we signed up for,
Before we leave,
This time on Earth,
It's so controversial.

The darkness has long gone,
It couldn't extinguish our candle,
It slowly dissolved itself,
Along with every man made natural disaster,
Like an out of date,
Ancient Alka-seltzer,
Within the clouded glass,
Of Mother Nature,
Our answers became clear,
All things must pass.

It's just another reminder,
Not to let someone else's fear,
Stand in your way,
Don't live in some one else's drama,
In their controversial cliché.

Those who once,
Called the shots,
Never learnt how to fire the gun,
The greatest wake up call ever,
Is when they endeavour,
To cover our sun.

There's no place to hide,
Who is responsible,
Is responsible,
Now that they're here,
Salvation is near.

The Cassandra Complex

What's the achievement,
That we're trying to achieve,
For all our dreams to come true,
After all we've thought to be true,
Has become disbelieved,
Are we all being played,
Into the very next dilemma,
By those with a hidden agenda?

If the burden of proof,
Is something we choose to ignore,
Then the whys and the wherefores,
Are lost with every excuse,
That has ever been viable,
What's the true cost,
If none of the corporations,
Are ever made liable,
For their actions?

How can we bring this tyrannical time,
This satanical time,
To an end,
Who's out there protecting the children,
Children don't need an injection,
For their protection,
Or for the protection of adults,
We have been lied to,
By satanic cults,
That are hell bent,
On keeping us,
Sick, distracted,
And unconnected.

We've been given,
A tasteless overdose,
Of bread and circus,
Designed to oppress,
And suppress us.

Our National Health Service,
Is over run with myocarditis,
Will it be the kiss of death,
Will the NHS,
Finally be sold off,
When it's unfit for purpose,
With nurses on strike,
And the most experienced ones leaving,
Nothing can stop what's coming.

We could retrace the steps of yesterday,
But who wants a future,
Of suffering and sorrows,
Furthermore,
We won't take any more,
One today is worth two tomorrows.

We're here,
To free ourselves from the repertoire,
Of entrapment,
To disregard,
What doesn't have our consent,
We are not here,
To live in any more fear,
Or ignorance.

We won't take a chance,
With gullibility,
It just attracts so much guile,
You know what they say,
Give someone an inch,
And they'll take a mile,
Living someone else's dream,
Is never worthwhile.

We are where we're at,
It's as simple as that,
Whether it's a clear day,
Or it's clear as mud,
We don't have to keep repeating ourselves,
Like we're Elmer Fudd,
Going around in circles,
Caught in the cartoon world of thought,
What's sought after,
Is found in the thereafter.

Whatever may come,
Is potentially perplex,
Here lies the illusion,
Of our Cassandra Complex.

So Lovely

Good golly,
We're now living through,
A massive rewrite of history,
Controversial as the bluebell,
That's really red,
We can rewrite the narrative,
The narrative of folly,
That stays within the Taurus field of thoughts,
Of what someone once said,
Let there be love,
As love is so lovely.

Grinding dust into dust,
Our trust,
Is the internal wind,
Within the landslide,
That we pushed aside,
We'll keep on turning,
The heaviest stones throughout our journey.

Why are the hardest lessons,
Learnt the hardest way,
Teachings that catch us unawares,
It's like the lies take the escalator,
While the truth takes the stairs.

What was so lovely,
About our yesterdays,
Will be engraved in our memories,
Who's reminiscing,
Remembering yesterday's dream,
That the dream catcher catches,
Whatever the theme.

Feeding those squirrels chocolate eclairs,
While climbing the stairway to Heaven,
Some of us may,
Have slipped on the stairs,
But we got back up again,
After each fall,
Without airs and graces,
With a smile that said it all,
Upon our faces.

It's never too late,
To face the day,
If we're finally feeling,
Like we're passed all that,
Here's a constant reminder,
To look up into the trees,
No matter the season,
Loving all life,
In this incarnation.

Why would it be throughout,
Every part of this book,
It happens to open up,
At this page,
It's not one to miss,
Take notice of this,
It's at each consciousness correction,
We begin to really engage,
To heal any ancestral lineage of lovelessness,
We could never buy love at any stage,
As love is beyond precious.

The eclipse,
Touches the lips,
Of those unbecoming,
Believe in the apocalypse,
Know thyself,
Until thyself is identified,
The lies from the liars,
Become tongue tied.

From the dialectic black light,
A star lights up for you,
You know what to do,
Something incredible is coming,
From the wrecks of this revenue,
Jacob's ladder retraces it's steps,
For your debut.

You are the one,
The one that is so lovely,
God bless the ones,
Who bring smiles to other's faces,
These are the days,
We join the dots between spaces.

These words have no bearer,
No price to pay,
In an unjust world,
It would be far fairer,
To just take Hell away.

Each claim is the claim,
That overcame,
For all to see,
When you look in the mirror,
Please look for you,
For you are so lovely.

In The Blink Of An Eye

In the land of saints,
And scholars,
In the land of truth tellers,
And liars,
No one has begun to tell ya,
In life's unresolved adventure,
That the pandemic is over,
It was never reported,
As it never started.

Life shouldn't have changed,
In the way that it did,
In not one iota,
But I have to say,
Everything changes,
And maybe,
It had to happen that way.

Within life's diary,
Of hypotheses,
What kind of sorcery,
Are we living under,
If we don't question all and sundry?

Yes,
There will be pain,
Yes,
There will be pleasure,
But it all goes by,
In the blink of an eye.

As we look back,
With hindsight's expertise,
To lock the majority down,
Is an unforgivable act,
Of draconian terror,
Abusive in fact.

The message at this stage,
Is for the detainees,
The time is nigh,
To recognise high treason,
To respect all life,
With awe and wonder,
Everything under our Sun.

Yes,
There will be difficulties,
But nothing is outside the realms,
Of extreme possibilities,
We will find our own discoveries,
When we go to extremes,
And we're here to do this,
That's one of the reasons why we exist,
As deep down we know,
One day all this will cease,
On the day that we find,
Perpetual peace.

Tragedy and melancholy,
Will never last,
Nothing is permanent,
It goes by,
In a blink of an eye,
It goes by so fast.

Everything is temporary,
As no one is certain,
With any certainty,
What seems to be,
The most accurate,
Could be so disillusional,
Fate prods the change that is coming,
So lets be,
Grateful, humble and thankful.

Change is indeed,
The one thing that lasts,
We all have many choices,
Choose in what you trust,
But over all,
Never say never,
Never give up,
To yourself be true,
Love all life,
As life loves you.

The Soul Survives

Something must of happened before,
Before there was anything,
Somehow into whatever,
We must not lose sight,
That in spite,
Of everything,
The soul survives.

History is like a broken record,
Until we show the World,
Our love,
Every laugh grabs hold of the soul,
Giving it the tightest squeeze,
As we go on gently with this,
With each tentative explanation,
Of each hypothesis.

Poems are written to keep us warm,
Through some of the darkest times,
Poems are written to kiss the scars,
Inside the depths of troubled minds.

Everything is linked,
The future's the future,
And arrives when it arrives,
Never disrespect your gut instincts,
The soul survives,
Our souls survive.

We're not here,
Just to remain in existence,
Living out a joyless life sentence,
Until death becomes us,
Trying to prevail,
Going over every meticulous detail,
From the ghosts of our past,
Our soul is the one,
The one that lasts.

So today,
Live for today,
As today was a good day,
How far do we get to go,
As all that lies down before us,
Has always been there,
Has always been on show.

It's never been that far away,
It was in,
Every little thing,
That we did today,
From who is right,
To what is right,
There's never been,
Just one right answer.

Perception,
Without correction,
Of our addictive behaviour,
Will never become,
Our corroborative saviour,
Nothing in life,
Behaves differently,
Without a change.

When we're aware,
We are already there,
Ready for the nature of things,
Open mindfulness,
Sees similarities,
As one and the same,
Fear is the sin,
God created Satan,
What once was all encompassing,
The Lord of the Rings,
The fame,
The shame,
The blame.

It's not just one way,
Or the other,
It's every which way,
From oscillatory,
We have to let go,
From holding on,
To Karma's involuntary infantry.

If life feels hellish,
Instead of heavenly,
If we're lost in this
Conceptual continuity,
Far too many lives,
Are somehow lived,
In painful purgatory,
Surrounded,
By what is,
Only temporary.

Remember,
Humanity's Trojan horse,
Holds more,
Than one disguise,
It holds no remorse,
Until we invert the inversions,
Break down the incursions
That have led us,
Off course.

We cannot resume,
Assuming and presuming,
After what's been exposed,
Under Tutankhamun's tomb,
This costume we wear,
Will slowly decompose,
Unleashing us everywhere
God has never lied,
The soul survives,
Our soul survives.

Somehow Into Whatever

Life's just one thing after the other,
But it's always right now,
So how could we make now any better,
By putting love in our hearts,
If we're not living whole heartedly,
What happens to be,
Beholds the believer,
And what they see.

It's the defining moment,
When you're in the driving seat,
It's you that's playing,
With divine orchestration,
What is it in life,
That we can't wait for,
Would it be more of the same,
Until all those what ifs,
Don't do it for us any more?

It's remarkable,
That we have any time for it all,
If we are living in a system of slaves,
Culminating in being occupied,
With an occupation,
Validating our interpretation,
Of an image,
That we think the World wants to see.

At what stage,
Do we,
Stop imitating,
At what stage,
Do we,
Become internalised,
With our own integrity,
At what stage,
Does good fortune,
Favour the brave?

We have the power,
To shower our love,
Somehow into whatever,
But not if we're waiting,
Playing our part,
With neurolinguistic programming,
For somebody else to show us how,
To follow our heart.

Back at the beginning,
We had authenticity,
We were all just beginners,
Not trapped in conceptual thinking,
Between being,
And becoming.

It's our internal conflict,
It's our illusion of self,
That'll ask for a caricature,
To build its role,
Somewhere in the future,
The hierarchy of needs,
Feeds the here and now.

How are heart bleeds,
For a conscious connection,
When the reality has gone,
It leaves behind our perception,
Has nobody told you,
How valuable you are,
Mentally, emotionally,
Physically and spiritually?

The darkness has gone now,
Now we are no longer left in the dark,
The corruption is clear now,
And we won't take part.

We are building a bridge,
Between the invisible and the visible,
Putting a little love in our hearts,
Expanding the truth,
Wherever we get it from,
Little by little,
Somehow into whatever,
To go on,
And on.

Fine Fettle On A Fine Day

For steam to rise,
The kettle has to boil,
Every kettle is a vessel,
Containing water,
For humanity to rise,
Their blood will have to boil,
Every human is a vessel,
Containing a soul,
Don't sell your soul.

The New World Order,
Has put it out there,
That you will own nothing and be happy,
But the only real possession,
We'll ever own is our body.

It's just the tip of the iceberg,
If they are trying to patent your body,
The wasp's nest has been broken,
Then stirred,
Towards the enslavement of society.

Don't be complicit,
In your own enslavement,
They have locked nations down before,
The walls are closing in,
With enforced confinement,
And fines from your Government,
They're working in lock step,
Against you,
Society was socially distanced,
Only to perish with this persistence.

Wearing masks while staying in,
The damnation of a nation,
Only happens,
With its participation.

We are not the same,
As we once were,
We will not become,
Our own saboteurs,
Those back stabbers,
And every false saviour,
Will lay right down before ya,
It goes back,
To way before,
Julius Caesar.

The outcome,
Will be different,
This time,
As we no longer consent,
To be governed,
By any tyrannous government,
With their mindless,
Mind control insanity,
They have to answer,
To every crime,
Committed against humanity.

It's coming home,
It's inevitable,
We're in it,
For the long haul,
Everything's changing,
Rome wasn't built in a day,
As it was waiting,
For the old Rome had to fall,
And this ain't going away,
As everyone's,
Conscious awareness,
Conveys.

With no beginning,
And no end,
Nothing,
Stops humanity's,
Wandering wayfaring spirit,
It's been,
As much about unlearning,
As it's been about learning,
When our teachings,
Seem auto didactic.

In life,
The toughest university,
Legend level,
Doesn't come easy
We're always evolving,
Praying,
Every soul will settle,
Soul searching,
Soul loving,
Feeling in fine fettle,
On a fine day.

Stargazing

Go easy on yourself,
Something's happening,
The Matrix has slowly been glitching,
That new moon has been projecting,
All over the place,
The waves hit the bay,
They won't shy away,
From those that they have to face.

Core values have an impact,
That's hard to maintain,
The great absorber,
Is the one that will never wane.

The Earth is not whirling around,
Like a fairground carousel,
But to be fair,
It is never still,
The truth is found somewhere in the factual.

Stargazing at so many signs,
Is everything linked to the astronomical,
Whatever shines between us and the ether,
Neither here,
Neither there,
Taking stock of where we are,
Who lays claim,
To the land, air and water?

As above so below,
Each star shines,
To express its true potential,
In the nature,
Of its own essence,
Within the palladium of our sky,
How ever hard they try,
Nothing can be hidden,
As every event,
Was meant to happen.

When we love what we do,
We will never ration,
The very next feeling,
Compassion holds passion,
When we occupy ourselves,
With healing.

As we stargaze with amazement,
Our present,
Has presented,
A picture of what's yet to be,
Guiding lights that we bestow,
Are like a magnet to the nouveau,
Of love.

The oath we take,
Is the oath that we make,
When we wish upon a star,
Combined with every combination,
Of the common threads,
Let's keep our chins up,
Let's raise our heads.

Stargazing,
A meteorite shower,
Has no power,
If we never bow down and take it,
So lets spread the word,
Until it's widespread,
Each and everyone of us,
Is amazing.

Beyond Coincidence

Everything is malleable like putty,
In the hypnotic hands of deception,
All that we are,
Us and the source,
Us and the creator,
Energy and vivacity,
Why do we listen,
Listen to any manipulators,
Let others tell us how it's going to be,
Between,
The third, sixth and ninth dimension,
Beyond coincidence,
Beyond illusion,
Between simplicity and infinity?

There's all kinds of mental callisthenics,
Under the weight,
Of someone's cruel statistics,
Words compiled to drive us crazy,
You're not the only one,
To ever feel lonely.

It's no coincidence,
That we're all clutching at straws,
So much is beyond expectation,
Than what we expect,
It's all happening right here,
In the theatre of verticality,
Without permission,
They're collecting information,
Without accountability.

Chaotically gold has gone,
From where it used to be,
Despotically driving more people,
Into poverty.

Lets shed a light,
On what can no longer be concealed,
In the battlefield,
We have to know our enemy,
The foes attacking humanity,
We're in for one hell of a fight.

They're keeping us awake at night,
With their programmable philosophies,
With their digital financial system,
Their experimental vaccination program,
Their bio-technology,
The quantum dot tattoo,
It's all there in plain sight,
Does anybody feel that this is right?

You may accused,
Of having a paranoid view,
But there are no coincidences,
When it really is all there to get you.

Within the pyramid of hospitality,
Morality can no longer be hid,
Lets lift the lid,
On every lie,
Let it all be revealed,
Lets exist in the real world.

For the shape of things to come,
No one needs authentication,
To prove their individuation,
Together we are immense,
Way beyond any coincidence.

Higher Love

Who wakes up each morning,
Exasperated over whom they've become,
Cognitive dissonance,
Is prevalent now,
So how do we go,
About saving everyone?

No soul should ever pass on,
By the hands of someone's deception,
When we're thrown to the wolves,
Higher love plucks at our heart strings,
Until we come back,
Leading the pack,
We all come back,
To face what's going on.

It's so hard to bite your lip,
While adorning each warning,
Trying to explain,
Every truthful tableau,
Screaming and shouting,
With empathetic pain,
Right in someone's face,
'Mate they're trying to depopulate,
The human race,
And that includes you,
And your loved ones too'.

No one is going to say,
I told you so,
When what plays out has run its course,
Whatever way we look at it,
Wherever we go.

Everything plays out in succession,
To leave a lasting impression,
Of reasonable force,
Leaving lasting remorse,
Reason laced,
With remorse.

When the people have had enough,
Of their smoke screen and mirrors detour,
This entire super structure,
Of civilisation,
Will be crumbling,
And all of this,
Won't play out safely,
If we pit ourselves against each other,
In civil war.

To call it as it is,
Is humbling,
As they try to hide,
So many hidden agendas,
All these hunger games districts,
Their 5G,
Fluoride in the water,
Digital I.D,
While they're drip feeding genocide,
As once again they divide.

So many battles,
So many fights,
Can our higher love intervene,
To ease,
All those sleepless nights?

After all those nights of research,
What do any of us,
Ever take away from the church,
From our choir of painful scars,
To the acquires of the stars,
Shining above,
What's been observed,
Is always served,
With higher love.

Pause And Reflect

Where are we now,
We all have to do something,
And as we do,
Why do we bother,
Holding onto our beliefs,
In some kind of chronicle order,
With he lasting reoccurrence,
Of yesterday's view.

When our path of least resistance,
Is no longer working,
What's so important about the outcome,
If we are holding onto indifference,
As we live through betrayal after betrayal,
While the real war carries on,
The war against humanity,
Without meaning or significance,
There's no longer,
Any justified honour.

As we pause and reflect,
Are we getting there,
Could we simply,
Let our yes be yes,
And our no be no,
Within the constraints of what we know?

As we have an obligation to the truth,
Who makes the claim is liable,
Who swears upon the bible,
The whole truth,
And nothing but the truth,
As we have been lied to,
From our youth,
By those who made us swear,
Is that fair?

The whole thing is suspect,
Riding along on life's ludicrous roundabout,
Life is the best deal ever,
But we've been so busy,
Busy externally,
If we don't go within,
We all go without,
We're all in this together,
Searching forever throughout.

We do it to ourselves,
We do,
Are we not entertained,
Until we entertain the thought,
Of what shall we do?

It's kind of laughable,
What's pushed forward as critical,
Crisis after crisis,
Here's another one to miss,
There's repeated patterns,
In all of this.

Within the patchwork quilt of blame,
It's always someone else's fault,
It's always the same,
As each and every kind of urgency,
Cries out an urgent plea,
For our own protection,
What do we protect to set ourselves free?

We are fundamentally,
Creating our frequency,
And that's the fun part,
Whatever we want,
Is what we want it to be,
Peace, equality, liberty or sovereignty,
We have always been the architect,
Of our very own destiny.

Magical Flame

It's engraved inside our souls,
Inside our hearts,
Seek and we will find,
Everything will have it's place,
While everything is playing its part,
It simply is a rule of thumb,
That it takes one lamp,
To shed light upon a stadium.

As we come to shake a spear,
At the wizardry of words,
The poet's hope and glory,
Their greatest wish,
Is to demolish
The insidiousness of what is heard,
Shine a light on daily miracles,
Demolish monstrosities,
Farewell my pretties,
Farewell.

Who has an idea,
Without an inclination,
Who has a drama,
Without a sound situation,
Who has a rule,
Without an expert's explanation,
Who cares to build,
Back,
Better,
Without a strong foundation?

The lies come tumbling down before us,
The walls come crumbling down,
For us,
The circus,
Has lost its life's distractions clown.

We are not forgotten,
We are not insignificant,
The boundaries that we hold,
Hold no further argument.

Those lines in the palms of our hands,
They tell their own story,
Those corrupt corporations,
Will never own you or me,
While standing on the shoulders of giants,
We can clearly see,
Our great observer,
Our truth preserver,
Would never let that be.

The Sun worshipper or Sun God,
Will bring the fall of Hollywood,
The holy wand will wave away the influence,
As we flood the labyrinth,
With our civil disobedience,
The magical flame is what we now clinch,
And it's one of civil resistance,
As we say no more of this.

The chapters call from the advent calendar,
As we see the bigger picture,
As we turn the pages of the book,
It's able to capture the rapture,
Of where we are right now.

As every secret reveals what we now seek,
Our angels come from different angles,
Arabic, Hebrew, Turkish, Latin and Greek,
Are all but one and the same,
As we now see the light,
Of our magical flame.

Gillick Competence

The illusionist,
Has more than just one trick,
Up his well worn sleeve,
To deceive is to mislead,
As to mislead is to deceive.

Virtually everything we know about drugs,
About their medication,
And its administration,
Is what the pharmaceutical companies,
Have told us,
Is what's provided,
Is so one sided,
If we can't discuss,
What's healthy?

The system covers up,
Their inappropriate guidelines,
Are we going to ask for transparency,
Or are we going to stoop so low,
As to blindly follow,
And drink from the system's poison cup?

Our health declines,
While doctors follow their guidelines,
Indoctrinated and over paid,
Just doing their job is no excuse,
To ask us to drop them and cough,
Is to induce abuse.

Our trusted physicians,
Are more concerned with their positions,
Future commissions and ambitions,
To question their suspicions,
That something might be a little off,
We the people,
Aren't going to let ourselves,
Get gaslighted by their protocol,
We just won't buy it,
It's time to learn how to heal,
And what is healthy for us all.

These so called authorities,
Make us the minorities,
Within their mix,
And that's the biggest gut kicker,
Wanting a quick fix,
While we're all growing sicker.

Heading for our own irresolution,
We're holding the axe,
Without holding the facts,
In our hands,
Future plans have been made,
By those who have been pre-paid,
Over our destitution.

How can we prevent,
Without informed consent,
A child's consent,
To medical treatment,
To any injection,
Without their parents' permission,
As scientists push the envelope of exaggeration?

Guidelines should be based on unbiased data,
It seems like most things get lost,
Sooner or later,
Lost in translation,
With some cold hearted administration,
Nothing's left that makes sense,
Untruthfulness finds its unrighteous position.

So how can a child,
In their defence,
Make a life changing decision,
With any Gillick Competence?

Culpability

Who is culpable,
Who is to blame,
You are,
We all are,
Once we're aware,
Life is never the same.

We all have responsibility,
To raise more awareness,
To everyone everywhere,
Our vibration is our immunity.

Who needs to be governed,
Who now wants to be governed,
By those who disguise,
What's really going on,
Far-sightedness goes,
Where far-sightedness goes,
There's no in-between,
What's seen,
Can not be unseen,
When it's all going on,
Right under everyone's nose.

It's their living hell,
Where the damaged ones,
Are all knighted,
As gasoline is being poured,
Over all the gas lighted,
And they are falling like dominoes,
Is each and every environment,
That we're trapped in,
The one that we really chose?

Are we all hypochondriacs,
At some level,
Due to their propaganda,
Where the bogus safety,
Only goes to serve,
Their own agenda,
Damaged people in conflict with themselves,
Inflicting their trauma.

Climate change lockdowns,
As they send in the military,
To where their only desire,
Is one that is mercenary,
It's not safe,
It's not effective,
It's not necessary.

Living within the pattern,
Of predictive programming,
It's exhausting,
Spiritually draining,
Who is now losing focus,
With the cost of living?

We have given them,
The benefit of the doubt,
Until there is no doubt,
Where is the love,
We're running out,
Of years,
Even though we're unstoppable,
We've had a gut full of fears.

Even though we're immortal,
Nothing is as it appears,
We came here,
To shed light on each situation,
For the next generation,
We know we are culpable.

The Becoming

Tearing this up,
Rip-roaring,
Inspiring,
As this begins,
Putting together the tiniest pieces,
It's mind boggling,
As something positive arrives,
Something negative ceases,
In doing what we are doing,
We are experiencing,
The becoming.

Right now,
Where is it that you're starting,
Are you drawing on life's experiences,
In every drawing,
Dancing with expression and feeling,
In the act of dancing,
It's like we're in some kind of movie,
But we're no longer pretending.

The educated empathic envision,
Knows how the story goes,
As your soul grows,
Into the becoming,
Even if right now,
You feel alone and suffering,
Start every action,
With the love of achieving.

Find the words,
To write your own poem,
To see what will ensue,
Listen to yourself,
To what sings from your heart,
Proclaim every word,
That really rings true.

There's always,
Different ways of seeing,
Out of the same mouth,
Can come cursing and blessing,
Otherwise,
What would be the point of otherwise,
If we don't harmonise,
With what we are creating?

The dawn chorus,
Is for us,
Whistling like a kettle on the boil,
The Sun rises for us,
Shining it's light down,
Warming the soil,
Beckoning each leaf into life,
The air that we breath is for us,
As we breath the breathe of life,
Into being,
We've been on a journey so exhilarating,
Self-aligning while we're becoming.

How do we come to view life,
Is it all playing out,
Like we're in life's play,
If life is a stage,
And at each stage we play our part,
Then we will also be in the audience,
Waiting for each experience to start,
Watching what we've created,
We ain't seen nothing yet,
Is it all activated,
Once we put in the effort.

Does our creativity,
Drive life,
Or are we being played,
If we're thinking too much,
While feeling too little,
Without committal,
Each character becomes brittle.

If it means something to you,
Then it means that you care,
Forever forward,
Into what's forthcoming,
To go on from there.

Every journey,
Is there to be explored,
Go out and be prosperous,
As each and every one of us,
Becomes,
What we are becoming.

Silence Gives Consent

Who's writing the script,
Behind the paper chase,
Which living man,
Holds the manuscript,
Of his own database?

Somehow from our own soul's sanctuary,
We were born naked without vocabulary,
Without the ability,
To express lament,
Our silence gives no consent.

We haven't signed up for this,
Lose the name,
To win the game,
The illegal fiction,
Of some corporate claim.

We were born an innocent curious child,
Until we're lead astray,
The more that we learn,
The less we understand,
It's the oldest cliché,
If we consent to joinder,
It's betraying who we really are,
So we watch what we say.

Everyone seems to have a smart device,
But who amongst us is smart,
As we all have to think twice,
If it's not from the heart?

We're so easily offended,
Mainstream manipulated,
It's stranger in a strange land,
When it's the television,
That they've befriended.

Who's being true to themselves,
While living within the Truman Show,
Without any real purpose,
Within the theatre of dreams,
Hiding in the darkness,
There are dark schemes,
Behind their themes,
In a simulation of perception,
We are beside ourselves,
Where nothing is what it seems.

We can't keep on turning the other cheek,
With no real voice,
Or intention to speak,
Leaving a dirty taste,
Inside our mouths,
The words we never spoke,
Lie their to ferment,
Our silence alone,
Gives our consent.

From this day on,
What happens we get to decide,
Our souls won't take,
What they've taken before,
Sudden adult death syndrome,
Won't be for those yet to come,
We have to expose all the lies,
Behind depopulation.

After finding our true voice,
We're not speechless any more,
We know we have to be on our guard,
For we are the guardians,
Repelling repent,
As we no longer give our consent.

Conspiracy Theory

What's it gonna take,
Until we all agree,
That the conception of a conspiracy,
Was from the Central Intelligence Agency,
Full of toxic corporate entities.

We're living in a corporate world,
Lost within their love for money,
Their one world government,
One world currency,
A microchipped society,
Towards the end of national sovereignty.

Who has heard,
Of a good conspiracy theory,
One that states,
That we are now free,
Not living in some dystopian slavery?

Where's the humanitarians,
Doing all they can,
Loving as they go,
Who says it's going to be okay,
Out to reduce,
The whole shit show?

Who listens without prejudice,
In a world where everybody lies,
After years of indoctrination,
Years of dumbed down education,
Something compassionate is slowly dying,
As everybody's suffering.

To heal the World today,
It's time for a different way,
Of looking at it,
As the Worldwide Confusion Corporation,
Just doesn't know when to quit.

The con still comes from the conmen,
Not only now,
But also when they say it will,
It's giving us the chills,
Human trafficking,
Human suffering,
The battle that has been going on,
Is as old as the hills,
War is war without retrieval,
The battle,
Is one of good versus evil.

What's bizarre,
Is anything and everything,
That we choose to ignore,
It's in our critical thinking,
What it kills it kills,
With geo-engineering,
With pills and bills,
Delivered by the Pied Piper,
If the bullshits on the surface,
The we need to dig a little deeper,
Without manifesting any more anxiety,
To pay the grimmest reaper.

Who can you now tell about tomorrow,
Without living through today,
We won't know the truth,
The whole truth,
Until every theory,
Has had it's say.

We're all the searchers of the truth,
That has been hidden for so long,
Until each conspiracy reveals the proof,
To right what ever is wrong

Wishing Well

The water holds the memories,
From open springs to overseas,
There's a million different wishes,
Wanting to come true,
Our Earth bled water,
Watch the water,
It's part of you,
It knows you well,
Spirit and substance,
Enhance,
The magic of the wishing well.

In this flippy floppy,
Topsy turvy,
World in which we sup,
The wishy washy,
Indecisive information,
Gets poured from a different cup.

In our toxic world of insubordination,
Nobody has jurisdiction,
Over the truth,
Grinding dust into dust,
Trust is the internal wind,
Blowing within the land slide,
There's nothing that can be hidden,
Trust your intuition.

When searching for the truth,
We find what is and isn't true,
As no one else can change it,
When it's all up to you,
As you readjust,
From dust to Atum,
From Atum to atom,
From atom to Adam,
Back to dust.

For who holds the authority,
On our Universe,
Every judgment is clouded,
As the dumbfounded,
Stand face,
To face.

Soldiers will follow orders,
Because that's what they're paid to do,
Take the money away,
How long will they stay,
Doing what doesn't ring true?

Violence begets violence,
Hate begets hate,
What hurts worse,
Boundaries or borders,
Or our diverse ability to relate,
It is never too late,
To ask for recompense,
For just following orders,
Makes no sense.

We can be the change,
The change that we seek,
The meek,
Will inherit the Earth,
Because they were never weak.

Humility holds strong,
In those who belong,
In a world,
That holds no terror,
The transformation is huge,
As grace pours out the deluge,
Of love,
From our water-bearer.

As a new dimension,
Wishing for attention,
Fuses together what was once parallel,
Soldiers lay down their arms,
To escape their living hell,
For there before the grace of God,
Go I,
For I see myself in you,
Therefore I wish you well.

Continue To Pursue

Ever changing,
Ever adapting,
In touch with the source,
Our energy force,
Inside of everything,
Everything in motion,
In so much as it happens,
Everything is happening.

Correspondence is nothing new,
Every divine deity is now in view,
Every new step that is taken,
Every truth pill that is taken.

Nothing comes too soon,
What's coming,
Nothing can stop it,
It's cause and effect,
Past reoccurrences,
From the poet's architect,
A marriage between the Sun and the Moon,
A marriage,
Between India and Egypt,
A ceremony rains down like a monsoon,
From the Heavens to the pulpit,
As each prophesy,
Once taught it.

We are here voluntarily,
To help humanity,
We are cells within the cosmic body,
Of the Universe,
Nothing is diverse,
We are an intrinsic part of all life,
And we effect everything on Earth,
As we take systematic,
Steps of understanding.

The long labour of deliverance,
You are the reverence,
Brought here to live wholeheartedly,
With the rhythm that rocks the soul,
Deliver us from evil,
Where past lives regression,
Plays no role,
Where misery,
Has no destiny,
Where reality becomes real.

You are amazing,
Chipping away at what's been calcified,
Prophecies have prophesied,
It's the greatest time to be alive,
It's the greatest turnaround,
The tide has turned worldwide,
To something quite spectacular,
As the old gives way to something new,
That no one can ignore.

There'll be no repertoire of resentment,
No resurrection of discontentment,
As everybody helps each other,
Flooding light into what once was grey,
We've paid the price of yesterday,
Our parasites have been washed away,
As we love the company,
Of one another.

There's no comparison,
As nature calls,
Everything is in you,
In what you pursue,
Don't rest on your laurels,
Do as you do,
It's all part of the journey,
Written way before you,
And way before me.

Nothing Beats Being There

Ever present,
Within the presence of now,
We can kiss goodbye,
To all those 'corr blimeys',
As we saw them coming,
Crazy energies are now shifting,
Something's brewing,
It's something else to ponder,
As we're realigning,
With our natural order,
Nothing beats being there,
When we're standing,
In our power.

Potent potential flows from our source,
An extraordinary unstoppable force,
As strong as it's always been,
Holding our life force in,
There's always the Sun,
Under our firmament of skin,
Powerful and free,
Free energy.

There's an act going on,
That we have to address,
There's no true bill of exchange,
In their corporate mess,
No one owns the land,
No one owns the air,
No one owns the water,
Energy is free,
It's what we are,
It's nature's law.

They hide free energy,
They hide the creator,
They hide more sources of resources,
They hide behind Antarctica,
They hide so much,
With false information,
Our lion hearts now roar,
From distant shores,
To our inner cores,
We are at the centre of creation,
And nothing beats being there.

There's a change for us,
It's coming,
An altered state of consciousness,
We are not liable to pay anything,
To any corporation,
The luggage is lost,
In their representation,
Somewhere in their misinterpretation,
Amongst their myriad of enhancements,
All contracts are null and void,
Relating to payments.

The game,
Is done and dusted,
The bailiffs are busted,
We don't need any permission,
To let ourselves go,
Free from corrupted scenarios,
No body collects any commission,
For their dysfunctional status quo.

The status is lost,
In the reincarnation of every soul,
Exploring the experience of living,
Without any imposed control,
To every living man,
To every living woman,
Come on,
Not giving up,
Is the gift,
That keeps on giving.

Our location,
Is found in our participation,
Our realisation,
Of each moment that is here,
Just like every moment,
It's the most important moment in history,
Inside our hearts is a travelling gypsy,
That wants to travel everywhere,
On a wing and a prayer,
Knowing that nothing,
Will ever beat being there.

A Hand To Hold

It's all about the words,
There's a poet lying dormant,
In us all,
As we're trying to uncover,
Every lie that's ever been,
As we take off our consensual overalls,
We owe it to ourselves,
To tie the laces,
Of our own plimsolls,
No one is going to walk in anybodies shoes,
When the laces are wearing thin.

The philosopher and the researcher,
Could twist the hieroglyphics of speculation,
It's one of the greatest cover ups in human history,
As we try to remember all the phenomena,
Our parapsychology,
Our psychic abilities,
Telekinesis is for those who free the mind,
Of its presupposition.

With closed eye lids,
We look within,
Everything is in motion within it all,
As everything is a constant state of is,
Nothing is more apparent,
Then what is.

We're in a dimension,
Within a dimensional realm,
Below a whelm,
That is transparent,
With a love that holds no judgement,
From a God that is universal,
Our unconditional parent.

Holding onto the exceptional,
That was once,
Set fast in stone,
Slowly gives way to what is crystal,
It's biblical,
And goes back to this,
The implementation of one's soul,
Is found within its own metempsychosis.

Through the tunnel of perception,
There is no wrong or right direction,
It's way beyond the physical,
The soul's ability to heal,
The Sun opens up her portal,
When the Sons of God,
Go back home.

It's as if the lost land of Atlantis,
Has landed in our laps,
As the guides from our ancient past,
Pull our silver cord,
Until it snaps.

Nothing is as it seems,
Looking back towards Tartaria,
Human rebellion,
Creates its own hysteria,
In the land of forgotten dreams.

The truth will open up every vertebrae,
Like the re-embodiment,
Of an unforgotten flower,
Somebody's somebody will be consoled,
As our lives flash by in flashes,
We all stand in our power.

Simultaneously we're beginning,
To see,
It's all in our DNA,
Travelling along with Yahweh,
Yeshua holds the hand of Fatima,
Everything is happening,
As everything was foretold,
We go on our merry ways,
We are beautiful, brave and bold,
As we reach out a hand to hold.

The Vortex

In our ever evolving reality,
We just want to uncover the truth,
Lift the lid,
On each transfusing perspective,
With all our presumptions,
And assumptions,
On what exists,
Way beyond our illusion,
Of turbulent twists.

There's a vibrational version,
Within the non-physical field,
There's a far greater expansion,
Of what's brought to light,
As night follows day,
Day follows night,
Within the vortex,
The balance of repetition is daily,
Concealed,
And then revealed.

The trilogy of stargates,
Is orchestrating our cyclic cosmos,
Opening and closing every vicinity,
This goes far deeper,
Into extra-territory,
It's another universal nudge,
From our holy trinity,
To keep us on the right path,
To what is hunky-dory.

The expansion is immense,
From whence it came,
It is unmeasurable,
Through summer, winter, spring and fall,
It dismantles the programming,
That was so damaging.

The news makes no sense,
Designed for the enslavement,
Of one and all,
From the north, east, west and south,
The archangels are throwing another curve ball,
From theoretical mouths,
It's the greatest vendetta of all.

As everyone,
Is creating everyone,
Don't allow your spirit,
To become,
Poached within the extravaganza,
Of entertainment,
Be aware of where,
Your time and money are spent.

There's fluoride in the water,
That circulates,
Calcifying one's brain,
These attacks come from many an angle,
Life as we know it,
Will never be quite the same.

We all have to HAARP on about it,
Until it goes away,
As it is all happening,
Right before our very eyes,
The High-frequency,
Active Auroral Research Programme,
Is damaging to everyone,
Whether we do or don't recognise,
Whatever they spray,
Into our skies.

Within our Petri-dish of poison,
The main players have fallen,
From the corrupt courts, banks, churches,
And their religion,
Where every rumour,
That was once misconceived,
Rose from the ruins,
To be believed.

Was it all just one big scam,
To control every woman,
To control every man,
Our souls are crying out,
With the echoes of hindrance,
Our circumstance died,
Within coincidence.

Has everything been purposely put here,
Like an unvanquishable cinder,
On the soles of our shoes,
As we go back over,
Our turbulent travels,
We pull on the thread of mystery,
To see what unravels.

Beyond those monoliths of magnitude,
Is another given chance,
To express eternal gratitude,
It's all been a pleasure,
In equal measure,
Thereof,
Experiencing the experience,
Within the vortex of love.

The White Shield

This projection of love,
Goes out to everyone,
Reviving a resurrection,
Of our forever freedom,
That all our fore fathers fought for,
They will not be forgotten,
In the role that they played,
Within this psychological,
Spiritual war,
The lions roar,
Comes from the heart,
Of our ancestor's losses,
Its awesomeness encompasses,
It all,
Until it all passes.

Say what you will,
And will what you say,
As we're learning to live,
Everything is relative,
With our own interplay.

Determined and driven,
Many are called,
Will it all be forgiven,
As few are chosen,
To find some peace,
Some day,
Wonders will never cease.

For every choice,
There's a consequence,
There's no sitting on the fence,
Of coercion,
Bearing witness to the monsoon of change,
Things always become better,
After things worsen.

Building bridges,
Shoulder to shoulder,
This involves everyone helping each other,
There's no real badge,
That could ever symbolise honour,
When this is only the beginning,
Of loving each other,
Guys this is far from over.

As we each play our part,
From heart to heart,
In our moral marathon,
We keep hold of the baton,
Before passing on.

New ways have been willed,
By the might of this pen,
It's a beacon of protection,
That's fairer than fair,
Wiping away the fringe of interpretation,
As we're aware,
Of the love that we share.

We're looking up and beyond,
Like never before we keep passing it on,
It goes further than far,
Further afield,
This unbroken bond,
We won't turn away,
Anyone,
Any more.

Shining bright,
Is our unselfish love of acceptance,
That's why we wear the white shield,
It yields the awareness,
Of one another,
Every sister,
Every brother,
We're all in this together,
Forever growing in our pilgrim's plight,
To reunite,
With the white shield.

Thank You

Hey you,
Thank you,
For all the time that you've spent,
Reading my books of lingering poetry,
It really means the world to me.

Poetry bleeds,
From deep in our hearts,
To open our hearts,
So that we can truly listen,
And go beyond the power of suggestion.

We're still in our infancy,
Ready to grow,
Balancing every possible scenario,
Breaking free from the strings,
That control our perpetual Pinocchio.

It feels like sometimes we're chasms apart,
Until it comes down,
To matters of the heart,
It's uncanny how trivial our differences are,
Thanks for being yourself,
And so much more.

Thank you,
God bless you,
For your patience and understanding,
For critical thinking,
In a World that so demanding.
Before this pen disappears,
Into the top drawer,
I just wanted to say cheers.

With this penultimate poem,
I wanted to make a difference,
By writing down what I couldn't ignore,
By standing up to evil,
We'll carry on living,
Thanks for being yourself,
And so much more.

Thank you,
To each and everyone of you,
To all those in the movement,
May we never stop moving,
Fighting for social interaction,
Without social distancing,
From facial recognition,
We will be ducking and diving.

Thank you for your beautiful smile,
Never wearing a mask,
For all of those memories,
All those laughs,
For the past, present and future,
For your continual rapport,
Thanks for being yourself,
And so much more.

Thank you,
For your courage,
To see this thing through,
You know by now,
That the World Economic Forum,
Doesn't give two hoots about you.

Thank you,
Is the least thing that I can say,
For not complying,
Just to make things go away,
Our compliance,
Only prolongs the painful decorum,
Until we can't take any more,
Thank you for being yourself,
And so much more.

Thank you,
For your unbreakable faith in all you do,
Questioning the unquestionable,
Searching,
For what is true,
With the free will,
That frees up your voice,
Knowing that your salvation,
Is in every choice.

As we look in the mirror,
To look deep within,
Clarity has never been clearer,
We need to let love in.

Thanks,
For being a light worker,
Spreading your light,
We are all so grateful for you,
You're a bit of alright.

Legacy
22/12/2022

Oh what a lasting legacy,
We could have,
We could have endless hope,
Or have another hopeless end,
After the fall of everyone,
We should of left it all well alone,
But don't wish your life away my friend,
Wishing you had somehow,
Lived your life differently,
As our Earth,
Quakes below repeatedly,
Not in fear,
But to repair,
The damage that's been done,
To all under the Sun.

What a blessed journey,
Breath between breath,
Between life and death,
Know thyself,
Until there's nothing left,
Until we all move along,
To where we belong,
For all we know,
As every forever beats inside our hearts,
For whom the bell tolls nobody knows,
Until those trumpets finally start.

When each time divine timing,
Consciously strikes,
Oh man,
How she really hikes,
With mystical synchronicity,
Sending shivers up the spine,
Full of energies,
Multidimensional vibrations,
Move throughout our core,
Like a new attunement,
With an old repertoire,
Shaking the tree of salvation,
We're here to save the children,
And you know it,
Just as you know,
You've read this poem somewhere before.

This is your life,
And your not here,
To just endure,
Or endear,
A life that doesn't make sense,
Or words without meaning,
You are the elixir of life,
Experiencing feeling.

After each revelation,
Lead us not into temptation,
From the profits,
Of the false prophets,
And all their illusions of debt.

Deliver us from evil,
From the hell that was never real,
When all things are considered,
They are only just things,
This brings,
Us to the third finale.

Hope you've enjoyed this poetical journey,
Take care of the insects,
Plankton and trees,
Our biosphere,
Is right here,
Lost in the breeze,
Don't let it all just turn to mush,
Benefit by becoming your own beneficiaries,
Investigate what's behind each disease,
Oh what a rush.

Farewell,
My unfair weathered friends,
Enough is enough,
Within our world without ends,
Love one another,
And don't sweat the small stuff,
Don't make forgiveness,
So impossibly tough.

As we come together with unity,
We're one big community,
I may be long gone,
Lost somewhere in each possibility,
Floating around within astro theology,
This is my legacy,
As it is everybody's legacy.

Love and be loved,
And above all,
Evolve, evolve, evolve,
All that once was,
Is never to be again,
As we let it all go,
Cheerio.

Third Time Truly Loving Unconditionally

Printed in Great Britain
by Amazon

25595614R00155